AF521605

ANTIQUES
YOU CAN AFFORD

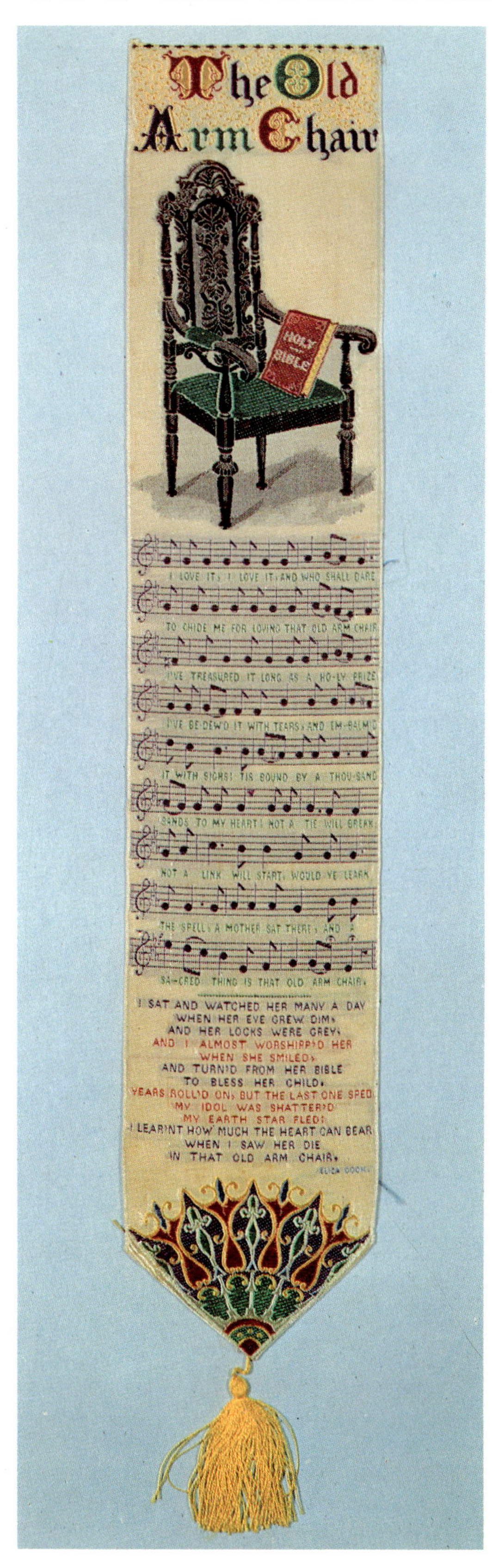

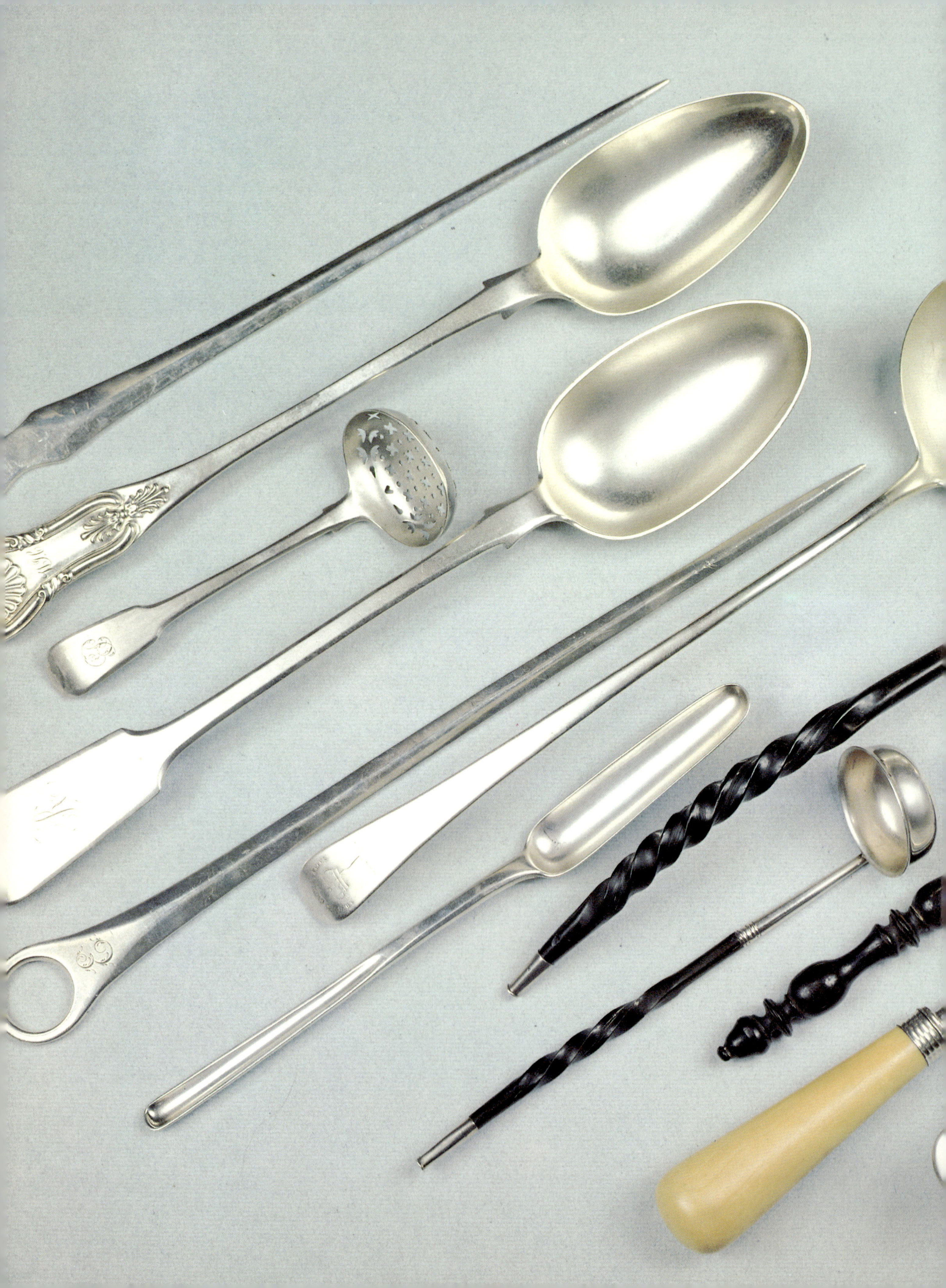

ANTIQUES
YOU CAN AFFORD

Bernard Price

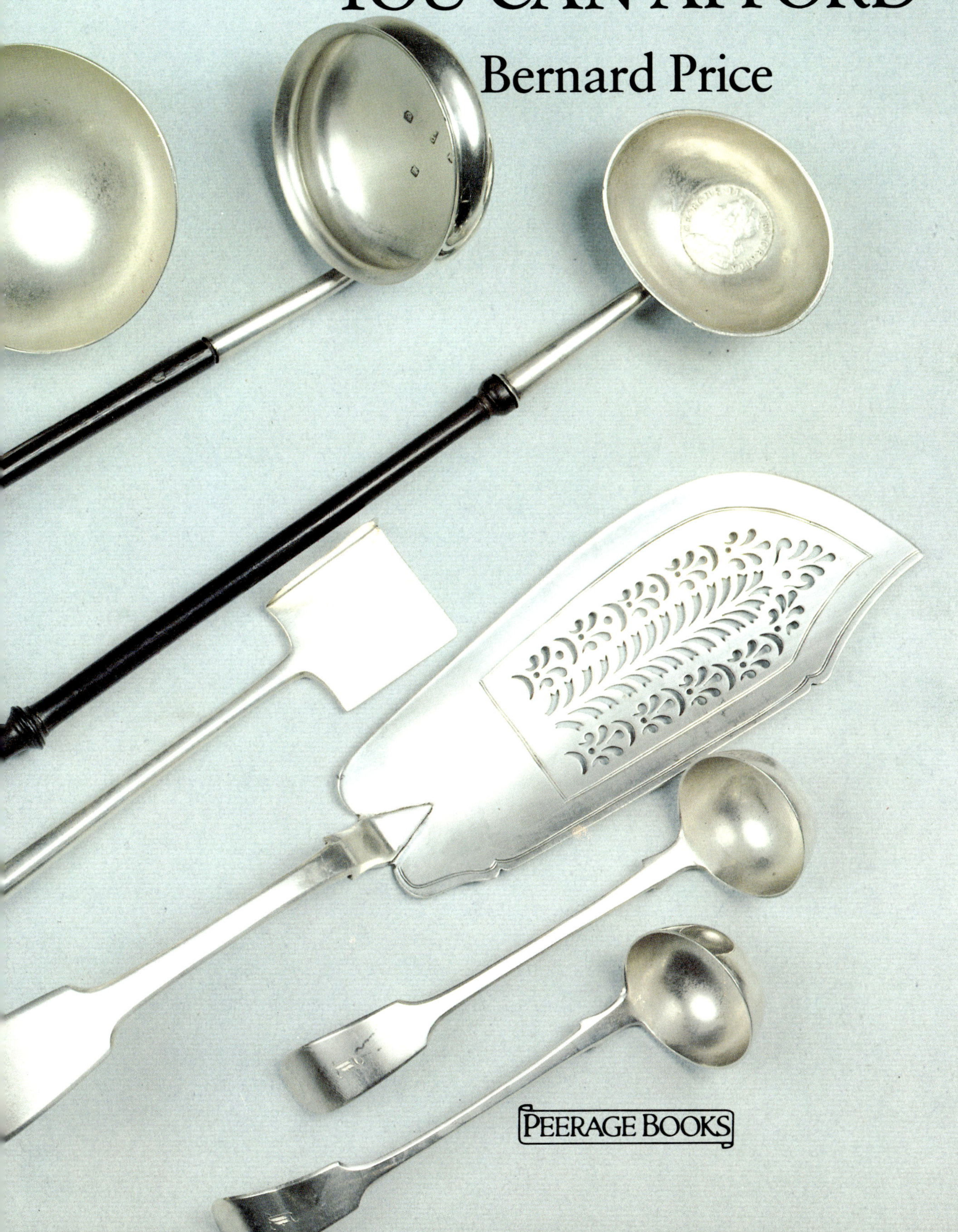

PEERAGE BOOKS

Introduction

My purpose in writing this book is not only to encourage popular interest in the traditional fields of collecting, which will always bring pleasure, but to provide some indication of the many new and frequently overlooked areas that are open to the collector. People have spent much time and money gathering fine and interesting objects around themselves for thousands of years, the Romans for example, were great coin collectors. Collecting is essentially a very personal pursuit, reflecting individual taste and interest. Some people have allowed their possessions to dominate their lives, which can only be destructive as well as saddening; most collectors, however, appear to have found the years of search in pursuit of beautiful and interesting things to have done nothing but to enhance and expand their lives.

This is not a book for the investor, but by the very nature of things most of the objects mentioned here are unlikely to become any cheaper in the future. All manner of collections may still be formed with a very modest financial outlay, success largely depends upon the combination of an educated eye and enthusiasm. Everything depends upon motivation. Money should not be put into antiques that cannot be afforded, on the other hand things sold cheap are not always bargains. Should you find some rarity at a price which is a little more than you expected, consider it carefully, there is nothing worse than looking back and realising that you failed to obtain what would have been your collection's crowning glory. The sense of frustration is the same whether spending fifty pounds or five thousand pounds. Never be afraid of seeking advice from professionals. I have never known a good antique dealer or auctioneer who failed to respond to a genuine enquiry from a collector.

To collect well and reasonably demands a mind of one's own. At least once a year a new book or television programme will appear on some such subject as buttons, bottles, or biscuit tins and, in a matter of days, a host of new collectors and amateur antique dealers will avidly follow in the volume's wake. So let your personal taste dictate what you collect and, by studying your subject, make it your own. Good hunting.

Bernard Price

First published in Great Britain by Park Lane Press and distributed by Marks & Spencer Ltd

This edition published in 1983 by Peerage Books
59 Grosvenor Street
London W1

This book was designed and produced by
George Rainbird Ltd
40 Park Street, London W1Y 4DE

ISBN 0 907408 71 0

Printed in Singapore

Contents

1	Porcelain and pottery	6
2	Glass	14
3	Silver	18
4	Paintings, prints and needlework	28
5	Stevengraphs, postcards and cards	36
6	Books and photographs	44
7	Jewellery	52
8	Coins and tokens	58
9	Toys and dolls	62
10	Metalwork	64
11	Domestic bygones	68
12	Horse brasses and rural bygones	74
	Bibliography	79
	Acknowledgments	79
	Index	80

Porcelain and pottery

This is the richest of all areas for the collector in terms of variety, world-wide distribution, and depth of interest. All over the ancient world magnificent pottery is to be found such as, for example, Tanagra figures and Etruscan vases. On the continent of America are found the painted pots of the Pueblo Indians and the exciting shapes of the vessels of the Incas. In Asia are the glorious wares of the Chinese. There are collectors for all the categories mentioned and for the products of every decade up to the present day. It is an exciting panorama to behold, and among the questions in the mind of the beginner must be where on earth one begins and how much it is going to cost. A collection will cost whatever you care to spend on it, and what you collect depends entirely upon your personal taste. While it is commendable to retain an open mind and to listen to the advice of experts, on no account allow yourself to be surrounded by objects that do not really mean something to you. Collections are born out of enthusiasm and knowledge and the one cannot exist without the other.

The terms used to describe the various types of pottery and porcelain are sometimes confusing and the following observations may help to illuminate and dispel problems before they arise.

Porcelain

This fine material is translucent, whereas pottery is always opaque. Porcelain falls into two basic categories, hard paste and soft paste. The word paste is used to describe the ceramic material or body of which an object is made. Hard-paste porcelain consists of a feldspathic rock known as china stone which is then mixed with china clay; when fired at high temperatures, between 1,300 and 1,400 degrees centigrade, the material fuses into a hard translucent body. This was the type of porcelain used by the Chinese and the Japanese and, centuries later, by Meissen and many other European factories, though by no means all. The famous early French Sèvres porcelains for example were of a soft paste from their beginning in 1745 until 1772, after which date they adopted the hard-paste body.

In the early years of porcelain manufacture successful European concerns tried to keep their porcelain formulas secret as industrial espionage was already rife. Hard paste was considered the true porcelain because it possessed the hard, bright appearance of the oriental examples. Soft paste was very much an experimental porcelain developed in various ways by makers who, although aware that fine basic clays were required, remained unable to identify the china stone that was used in the true hard-paste body. In Britain, factories experimented with ground glass, animal bone, ash and Cornish soapstone. The results of such formulas were undoubtedly porcelains in that they were translucent to varying degrees, so that each factory created objects that bore characteristics unique to itself.

It is through the existence of such characteristics that it has become possible to identify 18th-century porcelains that are so frequently unmarked. To recognize and understand the many subtle variations in the nature of the early porcelains is knowledge not easily won, but it is this very factor that fascinates and ensnares so many collectors for life. Handle as much porcelain of different periods and manufacturers as you can. View auction sales where you will have the opportunity of checking your own identifications with those of the catalogue. Talk to dealers who specialize in ceramics for they will be important allies in the building of a choice collection.

Glaze and colour

Hard-paste porcelains have a hard glaze that is bright and cold to the touch. The glaze is usually even, and its relationship with its body, is that of a very tight skin. Look at the foot-rim of a cup and the appearance of glaze and body can be seen.

Soft-paste porcelains have a softer glaze, some factories using considerable quantities of lead. The result is a glaze that feels warmer than its hard-paste counterpart and is often much thicker. Soft glazes on figure models may well gather and pool in the folds of garments or in the curve of a limb. The foot-rim of a soft-paste plate, cup or saucer will also help to reveal how a soft glaze tends to hang upon the body rather than having the skin-like look of the hard-paste examples.

Buying broken pieces of 18th-century porcelain that are beyond restoration can, provided they are cheap, also be a most useful exercise. It enables the beginner to become familiar with porcelain in a way that is impossible with perfect specimens. A chip or break in soft-paste will reveal an interior which has something of a granular texture. Similar damage to hard-paste discloses a surface that is glass-like in appearance.

Painted decoration is applied either over or under the glaze. Much of the early decoration on English porcelains was in blue and white derived from oriental originals, and was under the glaze. Decoration in enamel colours was applied over the glaze and the pigments can usually be felt with the fingers because they are on the surface. Do not confuse oriental decoration with oriental manufacture.

Rules of thumb

Porcelain figures with blue eyes will almost certainly prove to be of 19th-century manufacture. Only a small number of 18th-century figures have been discovered with blue eyes. Brown eyes in a good porcelain figure may well be an indication of 18th-century manufacture, but the characteristics of the porcelain should also be checked before making an attribution. Always beware of marks made over the glaze, as they may have been added at a later period; marks under the glaze must have at least been applied at the time of manufacture. Pottery figures of the 18th century tend to have hollow bases, those of the 19th century tend to be solid. These are not in any way to be regarded as hard and fast rules but it does no harm at all to keep them in mind.

The manufactories

The most celebrated of all European porcelain manufactories is almost certainly Meissen, the correct term for what many call Dresden. It was the Royal Manufactory of Saxony and was the first in Europe to discover the secret of porcelain production during the first decade of the 18th century, probably in 1708. Before that time all of Europe's porcelain had been imported from the East. The success of Meissen porcelain was due, of course, to the industry and perception of the alchemists who succeeded in creating it, and the brilliance of their painters and modellers. But their motivation had come from Augustus, Elector of Saxony, who spent fortunes on his passion for Chinese porcelain. There is a story that he once exchanged a regiment of cavalry for a set of Chinese vases!

The early porcelains of Meissen are remarkable for their quality and beauty, and the standard of their figure modelling is unique. Again, high values are involved but single cups, saucers and plates of the 18th century can be purchased reasonably and 19th-century examples even more so. Because Meissen is so celebrated there are many copies, most of which may bear the famous crossed swords mark in underglaze blue, or variations of it. The rare Augustus Rex monogram has been copied many times (see illustration).

◪ SÈVRES When this important factory moved from Vincennes to Sèvres in 1753, the crossed 'L's of the Royal monogram became the official factory mark with the letter 'A' to signify the year 1753 in the centre of the cipher. 1754 was indicated by the letter 'B', and so on, although the letter 'W' was omitted from the alphabetical sequence. In 1778 a double letter sequence began, starting with 'AA' and continued in this fashion until 1793 with 'PP' after which a new system of Republican marking was adopted. The reason for stressing the method of Sèvres dating outlined above is that Sèvres was much copied. Some pieces of hard paste were being made as early as 1768 when the date letter is 'P'. Copies, however, are usually found in hard paste and they tend to bear the earlier date letters. Therefore many items bearing a Sèvres mark before the date letter 'P' and in hard paste, must be copies. As a Royal manufactory splendid objects were made with little regard for

In the second half of the 19th century, porcelain was being decorated in Dresden by Madame Wolfsohn who copied the early and rare Royal Meissen mark of Augustus Rex. Legal action later forbade the use of the mark and these colourful, but otherwise totally inaccurate copies, have become known as 'Crown Dresden'

expense; the Sèvres pieces are magnificently painted and have an air of sumptuous quality. While such pieces are obviously of high value they are noted here because of the very considerable influence the factory was to have on later English porcelain design and decoration, the supreme example being the wares of Minton.

Various factories in the Paris area produced interesting porcelains, which may often be recognized by their use of considerable gilding which has a tendency to wear badly on the hard white glaze. One manufacturer who must be acknowledged here is the firm of Messrs Samson et Cie, of 7, rue Baranger, Paris. The company was founded in 1845 by Edme Samson, a china decorator. His son Emile (1837–1913) began the large-scale reproduction of early porcelains that has etched the name of Samson of Paris on every china collector's heart. Samson copied work from all the leading European manufactories, including earthenwares and enamels as well as porcelains. The original factory marks were also copied, and it is unfortunate that so many people, believing themselves in possession of a valuable piece of red or gold anchor Chelsea, have had their dreams destroyed by the eventual discovery that their cherished possession was simply a Samson copy. Some of the Samson copies also carry a letter 'S' as signature. Oriental wares too were copied by this Paris firm. New collectors of English porcelain will continue to be misled by the Samson products until the ability to differentiate between hard and soft paste is achieved. It should be remembered, however, that good Samson copies are now being collected in their own right.

Interest in all of the major continental factories is recommended. The 19th-century porcelain products of Moscow and St Petersburg are in more plentiful supply than might generally be thought. The porcelains of Berlin and Vienna have much of beauty to offer, although late products of Vienna can be very disappointing. Many of these pieces have transfer prints after Angelica Kauffman, some actually bearing her name.

It would be difficult to name any porcelain factory that is not collected. Only four English factories produced hard-paste porcelain: Bristol, Plymouth, Newhall, and pre-1820 Coalport. Although the hard-paste figures of the great continental factories have so much quality and sense of movement, the English soft-paste figures possess a charm that has made them the joy of generations of collectors. Good Derby and Bow figures are still to be found reasonably, but the Chelsea figures and those from Plymouth and Bristol are likely to be far more costly.

Among the more obtainable wares for the new collector the products of the following factories might well be considered: Caughley 1772–1814; Coalport 1796 to the present day; H. & R. Daniel *c.* 1822–1845; Davenport *c.* 1793–1887; Derby *c.* 1750 to the present day; Doulton 1882 to the present day; Goss 1858–1940; Minton *c.* 1793 to the present day; Ridgway *c.* 1808–1855; Rockingham *c.* 1826–1842; Spode 1770 to the present day; Worcester 1751 to the present day.

Many of the splendid hand-painted plates and vases, etc., that have emerged in the past century from such manufactories as Royal Crown Derby and Royal Worcester, Coalport and Spode, are of great interest and importance, particularly those bearing the artist's signature. The Royal Doulton figures at Burslem between 1890 and the present day are being increasingly pursued by enthusiasts who have noted their quality and historical importance. The figures withdrawn from production during the 1920s and 1930s are of special interest, many of them being fine expressions of Art Deco.

IRONSTONE was the name given to a heavy, strong body being produced in the early 19th century, of which Mason's Ironstone, patented by Charles James Mason in 1813, is the most famous. Oriental patterns are most commonly seen, with floral studies and relief moulded jugs. Some fireplaces were made of ironstone, but the most desirable pieces are those with hand-painted landscapes and excellent gilding. Blue transfer ware was also used for decoration.

PARIAN is an unglazed or 'biscuit' porcelain that in appearance resembles marble from the

OPPOSITE LEFT A selection of miniature items in Mason's Patent Ironstone China, with typical coloured patterns. The large vase is 20.4cm (8in) high, *c.* 1815–25

OPPOSITE RIGHT A Minton Parian figure of a dancing girl after the original sculpture by Antonio Canova, 1849

OPPOSITE BELOW Multi-colour printed pots and pot lids, together with a fine plate, from the Staffordshire firm of F. & R. Pratt & Co., *c.* 1860–70

BELOW Three most attractive mid-19th-century cups and saucers: (*left to right*) Coalport, Minton and Derby

island of Paros from where this fine 'statutary porcelain', as it was also known, takes its name. The firms of Copeland and Minton were the first to produce this white body during the 1840s, although Messrs Copeland were actually first in the field. Because Parian is mostly white (although tinted examples were made), it became disregarded in this century until very recent years when the value of Parian has risen considerably. Even so, attractive examples must be a good purchase.

The Art Union of London was established in 1836 and its members were especially concerned about the relationship between increasing methods of mass production and art. An annual subscription entitled members to take part in a yearly raffle or draw. The main prizes were usually paintings from the Royal Academy Exhibition. Eventually it was decided that lesser prizes of figures made of Parian would be ideal. Many figures will be found marked with the name of the sculptor and the words 'Art Union of London', or one of a number of other Art Unions which were to become established in Britain.

POT LIDS were also a product that emerged from the 1840s. The developing industry of potted shrimps and fish paste demanded containers, of which the shallow circular pots, with black and white lids advertising bear's grease as a hair dressing, were the prototypes. The principal makers of these pictorial pots were F. & R. Pratt & Co. of Fenton between 1847 and 1888, while others were the products of T. J. Mayer at the Cauldon Pottery, Stoke-on-Trent. It was Jesse Austin, employed by F. & R. Pratt & Co. as an engraver and artist, who perfected a process by which colour printing could be achieved by transfers, each colour being laid on with a separate engraving. Hundreds of pictures illustrating historic events and rural scenes, buildings, etc., have long made pot lids popular with collectors. Many modern copies exist, and old types were still being made at the end of the 19th century.

STAFFORDSHIRE FIGURES became popular in households towards the end of the 18th century. Cottage style ornaments already had a long tradition in the potteries and names such as John Astbury and Thomas Whieldon are renowned among collectors of the earlier wares. In the middle of the 18th century the Wood family of Burslem created all manner of fine figures, Toby jugs and plaques. Ralph Wood, senior, celebrated as a modeller, also achieved some of the most beautiful glazing effects to be seen on pottery, with lustrous transparent glazes applied by hand with a brush. Pottery of this quality is now hard to find but a collector who comes to know his subject and follows the market closely will inevitably find good 18th-century items in due course. Increasingly, interest has progressed through the 19th century to include the astonishing panorama of portrait figures decorated in strong colours. Although lacking the sophistication of the earlier

LEFT Staffordshire figures: (*top left to right*) Hamlet; a watchstand supported by three dancers; E.A. Sothern as Lord Dundreary in *Our American Cousin* by Tom Taylor, Haymarket Theatre, London, 1861; a moneybox of Shakespeare's birthplace; an ink pot of Mr Punch; a pair of lovers in an arbor, possibly Lorenzo and Jessica (*The Merchant of Venice*); a spill holder and clock piece (sometimes known as *The Elephant of Siam*)

BELOW The three transfer printed pieces mark the coronations of King George V and Queen Mary, George VI and Queen Elizabeth, and the Diamond Jubilee of Queen Victoria

porcelain figures they do parade a vivid gallery of personalities including kings, soldiers, and sportsmen, to actors and actresses, evangelists and even murderers! Once again modern copies exist and the prospective collector must familiarize himself with the handling of originals.

◪ TRANSFER WARE was one of the great commercial successes of the 19th century. It was introduced as a process in 1780 by Thomas Turner at Caughley. Unmarked examples of transfer-printed earthenware in underglaze blue are often difficult to attribute to a particular factory but there is no mistaking the interest of the transfer patterns depicting landscapes, cottages, castles, colleges and country houses, not to mention sports, animals, birds, and oriental scenes. Many factories were involved in the production of transfer ware and important contributions were made by Spode. Considering that fifteen years ago these wares might be bought for as many pennies as they are now for pounds, is a measure of their new-found appeal.

Hundreds of reference works are available on almost every aspect of ceramics, so the opportunity to learn more concerning any facet of this exciting and far-ranging subject is well within the reach of any china collector wishing to follow a particular interest. Books on marks also abound but, although most libraries maintain reference works of this nature, the collector will find an

ABOVE Blue and white transfer plate by Jones, *c.* 1835, depicting the signing of the Magna Carta; water-lily pattern plate, Wedgwood, early 19th-century; and the portrait plate of Josiah Wedgwood commemorating the Wedgwood Bicentenary of 1930. In the foreground are pots and lids by F. & R. Pratt & Co., *c.* 1853–60

RIGHT Art pottery vase decorated with seaweed and shell designs, signed Scott. Farnham Pottery, *c.* 1900

encyclopaedia of marks on his own bookshelf will prove useful and highly convenient, as will a handbook of marks that can be slipped into the pocket or the glove compartment of the car.

Art pottery

In the second half of the 19th century a number of art potteries began to emerge. Many of them pioneered new techniques and glazes and all of them were responsible for new designs. They were particularly motivated by such luminarys as William Morris, John Ruskin, and the rapid growth of the Arts and Crafts Movement. Most of them were small and varied considerably in output. They pursued the philosophy of the artist craftsmen, culminating in the individual studio potter who carried out or superintended the entire process from throwing the clay to final decoration and firing. Major firms in the pottery industry also encouraged the work of individual designers or artists, some of whom, such as Clarice Cliff in the twenties and thirties, have become famous. Among the studio potters of the 20th century the name of Bernard Leach is, of course, outstanding; fraudulent copies of Bernard Leach's work have already appeared on the market, which serves to emphasise his importance.

All fine pots by the leading artist potters clearly provide an opportunity for the collector. During the past five years interest in art pottery has rapidly advanced and values are rising accordingly. Collectors should particularly look for Martin Ware, that is, the stone-ware produced by the Martin brothers at Fulham, and at Southall between 1873 and World War I. Also the early decorative wares that come from Doulton of Lambeth, and particularly those pieces signed by George Tinworth and the Barlow family. Close examination of the earlier Doulton stone-wares, will, however, reveal most interesting and attractive objects by many other artists.

Names of other potteries and individuals include: William De Morgan, Mintons Art Pottery Studio, Burmantofts Pottery, William Moorcroft, Bernard Moore, Pilkington Lancastrian Pottery, Ruskin Pottery, established by W. Howson-Taylor, in 1898, early Poole Pottery, and Charles Vyse, of Chelsea.

All collectors should bear in mind that damage to ceramic objects, even when of a minor nature, will considerably effect value. Provided that damage in any desired piece is properly reflected in the price paid all will be well, but it is obviously important to purchase ceramics, whenever possible, that are in perfect condition.

Studio pottery by (*left to right*) David Leach (eldest son of the late Bernard Leach), *c.* 1975; Poh Chap Yeap, 1977; David Leach, *c.* 1975; Joanna Constantinidis, *c.* 1975

Oriental ceramics

The Chinese have a ceramic tradition reaching far back into prehistory. During the T'ang period the progress made in ceramic art was astonishing. Superb tomb figures of men, women, horses and camels, were potted with such skill and artistry that they stand among the unquestioned masterpieces of world art. In the 10th century, by using a formula that included what we now call china clay and firing it at a very high temperature in their already sophisticated kilns, the Chinese also discovered porcelain.

The fine pottery and the beautifully glazed celadon stonewares and porcelain belonging to the early Chinese dynasties, are sought by the museums of the world as well as by wealthy collectors. Over the past ten years some of the finest and costliest Oriental ceramics to come on to the market have been purchased by Chinese and Japanese buyers. Such a rarefied atmosphere is clearly not suited to the collector of more modest means, but it should not in any way restrain collectors from purchasing wisely and widely among the excellent pieces still available from the 18th and 19th centuries.

Trade and wars brought vast quantities of Eastern art into Europe from the 17th century onwards. On three occasions British taste and design became completely influenced by the East – in the chinoiserie of the Restoration, of the mid-18th century and during the late 18th and early 19th centuries. Great houses built Chinese rooms for which Thomas Chippendale designed 'Chinese' chairs, while the greatest example of chinoiserie in the world is undoubtedly the Royal Pavilion of King George IV at Brighton. The establishment of the East India Company, chartered by Queen Elizabeth I on 31 December 1600, had far-reaching effects for the next three hundred and fifty years. The clash of interest with the Dutch and Portuguese who had largely monopolized trade with the Far East, caused the English company to withdraw from Japan and concentrate upon India, so that the history of the British in India is largely the story of the East India Company.

Interest in the products of the East grew rapidly in the late 17th century. With the accession of William of Orange the fashion for collecting Oriental porcelain was largely stimulated by Queen Mary herself. This led to the designing of cabinets with glass doors in order to display the new and much esteemed 'china'.

LEFT A rare Caughley dish of fisherman's pattern

Chinese porcelain was costly whether it came to Europe by sea or by the more hazardous overland routes. Tea first arrived in Holland in 1610 when it was used as a medicine rather than a stimulating social beverage, but in the 18th century, when tea drinking became a highly fashionable addiction in Britain, the demand for porcelain cups and saucers increased yet further. Fanny Burney's mother once encouraged Dr Samuel Johnson to drink twenty-two cups in succession. The East India Company ships returned to the Thames laden with porcelain of all kinds, much of it made especially for the European market. Some services had the heraldic arms or ciphers of families who had placed their orders and patterns two or three years earlier. The reason for so much good Oriental porcelain in Britain is therefore explained, and even simple items from 18th-century armorial services are very much in demand today.

The first porcelain cups to arrive in Britain were in the form of tea bowls, so handles were a later development created by European requirements. At the same time it should be remembered that some of the 18th-century English porcelain factories continued making tea bowls into the 19th century, so the bowls do not always denote an early service. Chinese jugs with lips for pouring were made for export to Europe, as were all Chinese plates and dishes that have flat rims. The rimmed plate was intended for European condiments. Chinese plates made for their own use were of a rimless saucer shape and are known to collectors as saucer dishes.

Early examples of blue and white porcelain, such as those created during the Ming period, are rare and beautiful, but there are highly attractive pieces to be found dating from 1700 onwards. Much of this blue and white is termed Nankin because it was exported from that port. Similarly, most porcelain with coloured enamel decoration of the same period is often called Canton. Canton was once China's major trading port with the West, and Canton itself was full of enamelling shops decorating porcelain with traditional Chinese patterns and symbols, armorials and other European scenes and patterns for the export trade. Unfortunately the later 19th-century Canton designs with birds, butterflies and flowers become far too dense and overcrowded, failing to allow the porcelain to speak for itself.

Imari is a pattern used by both China and Japan with a palette of underglaze blue, dark red and considerable gilding. Such wares were first exported from the Japanese port of Imari by the Dutch, hence the name. The ware was actually made in the province of Arita and some of the designs copied the patterns on European brocaded materials. The quality of Imari falls away in the 19th

An interesting group of 18th- and 19th-century Chinese and Japanese pottery and porcelain. Note particularly the Chinese cup and saucer with armorial decoration, 1765, and the *famille rose* plate and tea vase, of 1760 and 1775 respectively. The *blanc de chine* lion dates from 1710, and extreme left, a Japanese blue painted saucer of 1740

century but it remained popular, and many English factories began to copy the Imari wares in order to keep pace with public taste. When the Chinese realized the commercial success that was being achieved by Japan, they too began to manufacture similar patterns using the same colours. Close examination of a Japanese example will reveal thicker porcelain, greyish in colour, with a glaze that has a muslin-like finish with tiny pin-prick holes. The glaze of Chinese pieces has a slightly oily appearance with a decided greenish tinge. The foot-rims of Chinese objects are also inclined to be somewhat rust-like in colour. When examining marks on Chinese porcelain a certain caution requires to be exercised, for Chinese potters frequently applied marks of an earlier period than the one in which they were working; this was not done to defraud but to acknowledge the skills of their ancestors.

Japanese pottery and porcelain, which for many years tended to be dismissed out of hand by European collectors, is now being regarded in a favourable light. Adverse opinion mainly grew through the massive exports of poor-quality porcelain that flooded Europe at the turn of the century. Fine Japanese blue and white porcelain of the 18th and 19th centuries may still be bought reasonably, and the late Kakiemon patterns, named after a great family of Japanese potters who have worked in Japan since the 17th century, are delightful examples of Japanese art. Painted in enamels, designs are executed in tightly painted naturalistic forms using grass green, pale yellows, orange reds and sometimes gold.

Many of the terms used to indicate the colour or main colour of Chinese porcelain are in French because French was the first European language used to describe such pieces at any length.

Famille Rose is the beautiful pink enamel colouring that was first produced in Europe and subsequently introduced into China during the 17th century. It was a colour that Chinese decorators really made their own and fine examples are eagerly sought after. It is a colour often found on Chinese export wares. Watch for plates, bowls, and dishes with ruby-coloured backs – these are very rare and are among the best achievements of the Canton enamelling shops.

Famille Verte Good examples from this green palette are hard to find. There are many 19th-century copies.

Famille Jaune is a term used for a whole range of yellows, most frequently used as a ground colour for a decoration from the verte palette. Genuine examples of Imperial yellow are very hard to find.

Famille Noire The so called 'black' porcelain. Rare and valuable. Decoration is often rather crowded.

Café au lait Used to describe the soft browns so much favoured in the 18th century either as a ground colour or when used in bands of decoration.

Sang de boeuf the term given to the brilliant ox-blood glazes used for their flambé effects.

Soufflé The attractive 'powder blue' ground. This was used under the glaze and was applied in powder form by blowing it through a tube.

CH'ING DYNASTY 1644–1912
Shun Chih 1644–1661
K'ang Hsi 1662–1722
Yung Cheng 1723–1735
Ch'ien Lung 1736–1795
Chia Ch'ing 1796–1820
Tao Kuang 1821–1850
Hsien Feng 1851–1861
T'ung Chih 1862–1873
Kuang Hsu 1874–1908
Hsuan T'ung 1909–1912

Glass

Any prospective collector of glass should exercise great care, for reproductions and pure fakes are many. However, all collectors have bought 'wrong' articles from time to time and, provided it does not happen too often, the lessons 'bought' and hopefully learned can only be of benefit. The first rule is to see and handle as many undisputed specimens as possible. All early English glass is now costly. Early attempts had been made to start a glass industry in the Venetian manner, but English glassmaking really established itself with the fine lead glass of George Ravenscroft about 1676. Ravenscroft glass is now exceptionally rare and valuable and the best pieces carry his seal of a raven's head. Yet during World War II it was possible to purchase such glass for less than £300. There were very few collectors during the early years of the war who had the courage to buy the very fine things that flooded on to the market, but fortune does tend to favour the brave and some of them must have been rewarded with great dividends.

The collectors of the 'old school' who would not have included a glass made a day after 1800 in their collection, are now few in number. English drinking glasses of the 18th century are superb, of that there is no doubt, but scarcity and cost encourage most new collectors to examine the products of the 19th century. Even so, some general comments concerning old glass and the 18th-century designs of drinking glasses may prove useful. Most of the old glass has a good 'colour', a very pleasing, slightly dark appearance. There may be slight striations like stretch marks in the glass (or 'metal', as glass collectors refer to the body of the glass). The foot of an old glass is seldom of less diameter than the bowl, and will almost certainly display some signs of wear, having been pushed backwards and forwards over many years across a table top. Some of the earlier glasses have a feature known as a 'folded foot', that is, a foot that has had its edge folded under like a hem. Such a foot no doubt added extra strength and also provided an additional decorative feature to the glass, for the fold can, of course, be seen through the foot. Some of the folds may be very narrow, but others will be as wide as 0.6 cm ($\frac{1}{4}$ in).

Many continental glasses were produced to English designs but after handling them few collectors are likely to be deceived, as the continental glass which used a soda-based formula is lighter than the old English glass and decidedly different in colour. Continental glass has a greenish tinge and very small air bubbles are often to be observed in it; most of this glass was produced in the Low Countries. While a collector will, hopefully, not mistake such glasses for English specimens, they are, nonetheless attractive and well worth buying at the right price, particularly when they carry good engraving.

Engraving which is contemporary with the manufacture of the glass is much sought after, but many pieces have been engraved at a later date. Buyers of engraved glass should therefore rely and learn from the established specialist glass dealers whose expertise can save the tyro collector so much heartache. Specialist dealers have been mentioned several times in this book, and the collector will find that many glasses (and the same applies to other objects too), can often be obtained more reasonably at such an establishment than in some small general antique shops.

Drinking glasses are generally classified by their stems, and fall into five main categories. These are as follows:

1680–1730 Baluster stems.
1730–1740 Plain stems. Air bubbles of tear-drop shape were often introduced into these stems; so were coins. Owing to its simplicity this stem is repeated in all periods.
1740–1760 Air twist stems.
1755–1780 Enamel or opaque twists.
1770–1800 Faceted stems.

English drinking glass with trumpet bowl, tear drop stem and folded foot, *c.* 1750. (*right*) An engraved and faceted continental tumbler, *c.* 1800

Engraving to commemorate historic events, particularly when it is of the period, causes the value of such glass to rise considerably. One of the most highly collected series of 18th-century glasses, and much copied, is the series known as Jacobite glasses which celebrates the Old and Young Pretenders. The majority of these engraved glasses were produced after the 1745 rebellion. The Jacobite emblems include the rose – in bud and in bloom – stars, forget-me-nots, carnations, caterpillars, oak leaves, lily of the valley, sunflower and butterfly. The word '*Fiat*' is also found, meaning, 'May it come to pass' or 'Let it be so'.

A feature that should always be looked for on old glass is the rough area left by a simple tool called a pontil. This rough and frequently sharp area is known as a pontil mark and it was caused during the handling of the object while it was being made. A metal rod, the pontil, was used to gather a globule of molten glass which was then applied to the centre of the base of whatever object was being manufactured. When the task was finished the rod was broken away and the scar was created. In the 19th century it increasingly became the practice to grind and polish the pontil mark away, leaving a small smooth depression in the base. The foot of an old glass tends to be high, that is, it may be domed or otherwise raised, rather like an inverted saucer. This kept the pontil clear of the surface on which the glass stood and enabled it to stand firm. For this reason a glass that is standing on a completely flat foot cannot be an old example.

A number of excellent books may be obtained that deal with all periods of glass production from the 17th century to the present. Because of the interest now being shown in Victorian glass, some of the types now being collected are listed below:

Cranberry glass

Although called 'ruby glass' by some, cranberry glass tends to be various shades of rose pink rather than rich ruby. Popular through much of the Victorian era it enjoyed a great revival of interest during the late 1960s in Britain and in North America. Jugs, glasses and bowls are in plentiful supply but good vases and epergnes are

A painted Burmese glass vase; a Burmese glass fairy light; a frilled cranberry glass bowl and cover; a cranberry decanter with handle and stopper; a Nailsea flask, early 19th-century; and a mallet shaped Bristol blue glass decanter, early 19th-century

more difficult to find. Pinched glass ornament is often used on the decorative examples and clear glass was frequently used for bases, handles and rims. Powder bowls, sugar bowls, salt cellars and decanters are very attractive in this colour and many such pieces were produced at Stourbridge, but the large quantity of cranberry glass that still exists would indicate that a considerable amount was later supplied by glass manufacturers on the Continent. Some cranberry glass bears the Mary Gregory style of decoration.

Mary Gregory glass

This is the name given to a style of decoration, mainly of children and somewhat reminiscent of Kate Greenaway, amid landscapes of trees and flowers pursuing butterflies and flying kites. The real Mary Gregory was an outworker decorator employed by the Boston and Sandwich Glass Company, of Massachusetts, and she was attributed with devising the decoration that bears her name. It is now known, however, that a glass factory in Jablonec, in what is now Czechoslovakia, was first to introduce such designs. The ornament was applied in white enamels on clear or tinted glass and gilding was used from time to time. The main period of production was between 1850 and 1890, although many later pieces are seen. Quality varies greatly among the Mary Gregory pieces. Flesh tints are often applied to the hands and faces of the later work. Some pieces are of very recent origin but with these, although the style has been retained, the sense of the 19th century is missing and the children's features have an air of modernity that is unmistakable.

Fairy lamps

In the second half of the 19th century, summer fêtes and Christmas shows were often given the added illumination and attraction of hundreds of glass fairy lamps. These lamps of coloured glass, shaped like old honey pots and lit by a night-light, were increasingly used during Victorian festivities and in particular for the Golden and Diamond Jubilee celebrations of 1887 and 1897. Once common, they now have to be searched for but they remain very cheap. Half a dozen fairy lamps of different colours would form a representative and very attractive collection.

Burmese glass

Experiments were continually being made in the second half of the 19th century with oxides and other techniques for new methods of colouring glass. The Mount Washington Glass Company, of New Bedford, Massachusetts, developed a method for the shading of colour within a glass object. This was achieved by the use of certain metallic oxides and a technique of reheating and submitting sections of the glass to varying temperatures. This resulted in a series of beautifully shaded and delicate colours. The Burmese glass, as it was called, of the Washington Glass Company, was a semi-opaque satin-surfaced glass shading from a fine pink to a most delicate tone of primrose yellow. Examples with trailing-leaf patterns are particularly attractive. The process was patented in America in 1875 and then in England six months later. Thomas Webb & Sons obtained the licence to manufacture in Britain, and because

Art nouveau and 19th-century coloured glass including a flashed glass jar and stopper; a pair of Lalique vases; red and yellow Mary Gregory glass; Amberina glass; and two fine examples of pressed glass by Sowerby's of Gateshead

examples of the glass had been accepted by Queen Victoria, Webbs promptly advertised their product 'Queens Burmese Ware'.

Amberina

This was the name given to glass with colours shading from red to amber. All Victorian glass with the colouring techniques described is well worth collecting.

Bristol Blue

Most glass factories in Britain manufactured coloured glass during the late 18th and 19th centuries. Bristol produced fine examples, but accurate attributions are difficult. Blue glass, obtained by the use of cobalt oxide, is the most popular colour of all. Specimens with a gilded decoration of foliage, or words on decanters such as 'brandy' or 'rum', are much sought after. Glass signed by the Lazarus family is rare.

Flashed glass

As its name possibly suggests, flashed glass was a cheaper version of cameo or cased glass, in that it was dipped in molten coloured glass, thus providing a thin skin of colour that could be cut or etched with ease. Many Victorian scent bottles were decorated in this way. Cameo glass is a glass vessel of one colour overlaid with a casing or casings of one or more other colours. These different layers were then cut through like a cameo to reveal the coloured layers.

Pressed glass

This process was first developed in America. Instead of blowing glass into a mould, molten glass was dropped in and pressed into shape by a workman simply pulling a lever. It was a method that raised the production rates of everyday wares astonishingly and later some interesting coloured glass was made by this method. Among the most collectable of the pressed glass decorative pieces are those manufactured by the firms of Sowerby's Ellison Glass Works, Gateshead, George Davidson also of Gateshead, and the factory of Henry Greener of Sunderland. These factories were among the few who marked their goods. The marks are not always easy to find, and hand as well as eye may be needed to detect the relief mark on the inside of, say, a small vase or basket. Sowerby's used the mark of a peacock's head; Greener the mark of a demi-lion holding a battle-axe; and Davidson the mark of a demi-lion rising from a coronet.

Slag glass, so called because the slag skimmed from molten iron or steel before it was poured, was found to mix with clear glass and form a very hard and attractive material. Although slag glass of single opaque colours is not difficult to find, the examples of a heavily marbled effect are proving widely popular with collectors. Slag glass was ideally suited to pressed glass methods of production.

It is the cased, cameo glass, Burmese glass, the quilted glass consisting of an opaque body with an incised pattern covered with an outer coloured casing, opaline glass, and glass influenced by the Arts and Crafts Movement, that creates most attention in the saleroom. All well-designed Victorian glass is worthy of a collector's time and further study.

Neither should the colourful curiosities of Nailsea be neglected. Glass bells, pipes, walking sticks, and flecked glass rolling-pins are all part of the wide range of products that come from this West Country factory that was manufacturing from the late 18th century until 1873.

Although it was made in this century, some collectors have been attracted by Carnival Glass, an American form of pressed glassware with a highly iridescent finish. It is found in a range of colours and those having raised motifs on the inner face of an object are perhaps the most interesting. Marigold glass is a name given to specimens of a gold colouring. Three American factories were the producers of Carnival glass: The Northwood Glass Co., Penn; The Imperial Glass Co. of Ohio; and Fentons Art Glass Company of West Virginia who also make modern examples today.

A pair of rare white pressed glass mugs depicting Punch and Judy

Art Nouveau glass

Art Nouveau glass by leading makers such as Tiffany in America, Emile Galle in France, or other makers of that period are clearly great prizes for the glass collector but values are obviously high. It is included for mention here for the simple reason that small and delightful examples of Art Nouveau work continue to turn up in surprising places, awaiting the knowledgeable collector. Much of Gallé's work is signed, the signature often appearing in relief as part of the raised decoration.

Silver

Anyone who wishes to collect English silver must first understand the system of English hallmarking, that is, the series of marks applied by an Assay Office to denote the provenance of an object, its maker, silver content, and its date of assay. Under British law, before any piece of silver may be sold it must first be hallmarked as such. English hallmarking has created the finest system of quality control in the world. From it a purchaser will understand precisely what is being sold, and will also know that the silver content of whatever the article might be will also be the highest in the world. When politicians began to negotiate for the entry of Britain into the Common Market, firm measures were taken to ensure that the English silver standard would be maintained at its high level and not reduced to the lower standard of the rest of Europe. Two standards of silver exist in Britain: Sterling silver and Brittania silver. The early silversmiths rapidly discovered that pure silver was far too soft for general use, but the addition of a small quantity of copper was found to create a far more satisfactory alloy. Copper does not affect the colour of the silver in any way but simply toughens it for general use. It is because the silver and copper alloy was so successful that it was open to abuse and sheer fraud. Without careful analysis it is impossible to tell the proportions of silver and copper being used. The appearance of a silver object to most people is the same whether it contains forty per cent pure silver or ninety per cent. The problem was realized at a very early period, and in 1238 an Ordinance of Henry III was already setting standards for gold and silver, and 'six discreet goldsmiths' were given the task of supervision. The first method used to discover the quantity of base metal present in silver was to melt it in a furnace known as a cupel, the passage of air over the molten metal causing base metals present to become oxidized. Thus, through melting and skimming the oxides off the top, the quality of the metal could be determined. This was a process probably first used by the Chaldeans as long ago as 2500 B.C.

Silver standards

◪ STERLING SILVER is the name given to silver of a standard fineness of 92.5 parts silver to 7.5 parts copper or other metal. The term 'sterling' is undoubtedly ancient but its precise origin is not entirely certain. Authorities ascribe its derivation to the Hansa merchants or Easterlings, so-called because they came from Eastern Europe, and supplied silver of this fineness from mines in Northern Germany. When King John invited German silversmiths to England to create a standard for the silver coinage, also to be applied to wrought plate, the fineness of silver mentioned above became confirmed and silver coins themselves became known as Easterleys or Easterlings. The derivation from this quarter would seem most likely, but the four starlings that appear on the coat of arms of Edward the Confessor have also been raised as a possible source.

◪ BRITANNIA SILVER, also called new sterling, increased the fine silver content yet further which produced a metal that is decidedly softer. It consists of 95.84 parts fine silver. The Britannia standard is not widely used and is seldom adopted for articles likely to be in regular use. It is far more commonly used for special presentation pieces. The silver of the new standard was introduced following the increasing practice of coin clipping, which involved cutting very small pieces off the edge of silver coins – easily done when the coinage was struck by hand. With new methods of coin production during the reign of Charles II any clipping of coins was immediately obvious, but

Britannia silver tea caddy with a bold hallmark clearly showing Britannia and the 'lion's head erased', London 1918, Crichton Brothers

dishonest silversmiths, faced with a shortage of silver, were ready to pay good prices for clippings and clipped coins in order to melt them down for the making of wrought plate. The government made efforts to call in the old coinage in order to stop its abuse but the problem was not solved until the introduction of the new standard of 95.84 per cent. In 1720 the sterling standard was re-introduced and the Britannia standard was made optional, a situation that has existed through to the present day. On Britannia silver the standard mark of the lion passant is replaced by the seated figure of Britannia. A further mark of a lion's head, known as 'lion's head erased' is also included, which shows a profile of a lion's head with ragged mane.

Principal marks

◩ THE LEOPARD'S HEAD. Since 1544 this has been the town mark of London, but it was first used on silver in 1300 when a statute of Edward I set out that silver was not to be sold unless assayed and struck with a mark by the wardens of the Guilds of Goldsmiths. This mark was known as the King's mark as it portrayed the head of a lion. The lion was familiar in heraldry if not on silver and as, in heraldic language, the lion's head was described as 'Leopart' it became known as the 'leopard's head'. From 1478 to 1821 the leopard's head carried a crown.

◩ THE MAKER'S MARK In 1363 the leopard's head was joined by the mark of the gold or silversmith. This was yet a further guarantee of the fineness of the silver and quality of workmanship, for the individual mark of the silversmith made him responsible for any object submitted to the Guild. Initially each maker was represented in his mark by a sign, usually his shop sign, but later this was changed to initials.

◩ THE DATE LETTER Just as the word 'alloy' sprang from *à la loi* meaning 'according to the law', so the word 'assay' comes from the French *assai* or 'examination'. The mark was a letter of the alphabet which was changed annually on a set date when the warden responsible for the assay was changed. First the silversmith was held responsible for his work by the addition of his mark, and now the warden could be identified in the same manner should he allow below-standard silver to pass assay. The mark was first known as the 'Touch Warden's Mark'. Each series of letters used had a new style of lettering and a new shape of shield surrounding it. Not all the letters of the alphabet were used and each Assay Office had its own style of letters. When wishing to determine the date of assay of any given piece of silver it is necessary to obtain a book of hallmarks and find the correct date letter under its own assay office.

◩ THE STANDARD MARK Often termed the lion mark by collectors, this mark was introduced as a standard mark to replace the leopard's head which then became the London town mark. The reason for this change was to renew badly needed confidence in the silver standard. Although it had remained unchanged so far as wrought silver plate was concerned, the silver coin of the realm had become seriously debased. Not surprisingly, the Goldsmiths' Company was worried when the silver content of coin fell to fifty per cent or less of face value during the reign of Henry VIII. The standard mark, later reinforced by law, depicted a lion as though walking left past the spectator and with one paw raised; again, to use the heraldic term, it was described as a 'lion passant'.

◩ THE DUTY MARK, OR SOVEREIGN'S HEAD On 1 December 1784 the four silver hallmarks described above were joined by a fifth. It took the form of a profile of George III and it indicated that a new tax imposed on silver had been paid. For the first year of its use the royal profile had the unique distinction from all other marks of having been struck incuse or intaglio, that is, it has the effect of being sunken. Other hallmarks have a raised cameo effect. Both the tax and the duty mark were not abolished until 1890.

London hallmark bearing the Sovereign's head, or duty mark, stamped incuse for the year 1795. (*below*) Edinburgh hallmark for the year 1848

Other marks

◩ THE DRAWBACK MARK This mark is seldom seen and is an incuse representation of a standing figure of Britannia. It was in use between December 1784 and July 1785 when it was withdrawn. The mark came into use when silversmiths claimed 'drawback' of duty on exported silver. The mark was not considered desirable because it was added to silver objects after they had been finished. Other hallmarks are applied before final finishing. Instead of the drawback mark the repayment of duty paid was claimed against invoices.

◩ THE JUBILEE MARK This special and very attractive mark shows the profile heads of King George V and Queen Mary. It was a voluntary mark to commemorate the Silver Jubilee and was used between 1933 and 1935.

The Silver Jubilee of 1977 was commemorated by such a mark, and it shows the profile head of Queen Elizabeth II.

CORONATION MARK Between 1952 and 1953 silversmiths sending work for assay could choose this additional mark. It shows the profile crowned head of Queen Elizabeth II.

Assay towns

So far, mention has only been made of London as a place of assay, indicated in the hallmark as the leopard's head. Goldsmiths' guilds, however, were established in many parts of Britain with the right to mark their local wares. These included Chester, York, Exeter, Bristol, Norwich, Newcastle, Salisbury, Lincoln, Coventry, Plymouth, Dublin, Birmingham, Sheffield, Edinburgh, Glasgow, Aberdeen, Taunton, Barnstaple, Hull, Inverness, Dundee, Elgin, Leeds, The Channel Islands, and many others. Silver from the early provincial assay offices has been collected for many years and this tends to be a somewhat costly field.

The only major assay offices open in more modern times have been London, Edinburgh, Glasgow, Chester, Sheffield, Birmingham, Newcastle and Dublin. Of these eight assay offices only four now remain:

London Leopard's head as town mark, appearing on gold, silver and platinum.
Birmingham Anchor as town mark, appearing upright on silver and horizontal on gold.
Sheffield York rose as town mark, appearing on gold, silver and platinum. Before 1975 the town mark was a crown.

The Assay Offices of Birmingham and Sheffield were both established in 1773, largely due to the efforts of the industrialist Matthew Boulton who lead the manufacturers of wrought plate in these towns in presenting their case to Parliament. During the weeks while this was taking place, it is believed that the Crown and Anchor Tavern in the Strand was the regular meeting place of the petitioners, and was to provide the new assay offices with their town marks of Crown and Anchor!

Edinburgh A three-towered castle as town mark, appearing on both gold and silver.

(Both Edinburgh and Glasgow used a thistle as a standard mark. Since the establishment of the Irish Free State in 1922, only marks struck in Dublin prior to 1 April 1923 are recognized as approved British hallmarks. The Dublin town mark is a figure of Hibernia seated by a harp.)

Foreign silver

Foreign silver must be assayed for marking. Needless to say, large quantities of unmarked wrought plate from the Far East, Middle East, and South America exist in Britain. Very little of this silver will be of equal standard and it is therefore no longer permissible to sell such objects as silver.

From 1876–1904 foreign silver of the required standard was hallmarked in the usual way, but with the addition of a capital F in an oval. Between 1904 and 1906 London marked foreign silver with 'the sun with rays', Sheffield with 'two arrows crossing two more', and Glasgow with 'the bishop's mitre'. From 1906 the designs were altered, and as well as the usual hallmarks the following marks were added:

London Sign of constellation Leo.
Birmingham An equilateral triangle.
Sheffield Sign of constellation Libra.
Chester An acorn with two leaves.
Edinburgh St Andrew's Cross.
Glasgow The letter F doubled to form a key pattern.

Buying silver

It is hoped that the above marks will be found useful in explaining the otherwise baffling symbols to be found on English silver. From the marks described it will be seen that it is possible to identify the silversmith who made any particular piece of silver, where and when it was assayed, plus the quality of the silver. As always there is no substitute for handling the items you wish to collect, and in handling silver the hallmarks will eventually become familiar and the collector will find their interpretation second nature.

Before listing a number of silver items that may still be obtained without too great a financial outlay, it may be helpful to make some general observations on the subject. First of all it should be remembered that a true collection is not merely many objects gathered together in one place. Each object ideally requires to be related in some way with its companions and once you have three such objects you have the makings of a collection. In other words a collection should tell a story, each piece chosen as carefully as words. Above all it is quality that is important – anyone can bring together second, third or fourth rate pieces – but it takes patience, appreciation and knowledge to obtain the best. In the market-place that has developed in art, craftsmanship and beauty during this second half of the 20th century few things may be obtained cheaply, but how much better to own a few fine things than a number of indifferent objects. Many people today purchase silver and other antiques purely for investment, but a steady growth in value over a number of years can never be guaranteed. If, however, substantial profits are to be made in this way, they will come because of quality and that rare knowledge that knows not only when and what to buy, but also when to sell.

I hope that the readers of this book will buy because they find sheer delight in the objects they wish to gather about them in their homes. Such people also tend to make good investments as

For the collector of small silver the range and variety is never ending. While some objects have now become cabinet pieces, such as the candle snuffer (*right front*), or the shoe shown here, much of it has the attraction of also being useful and adding charm to daily life. Other items include: (*left of centre*) a baby's feeder or pap-boat; (*right of the shoe*) a scent bottle; (*centre*) large strainer spoon; (*front left*) needle case; (*front centre*) an egg-shaped nutmeg grater

well. Time spent in learning as much as possible concerning a chosen subject is never wasted. There are now more books for general and specialist readers on antiques than at any time in history; the only problem is in reaching a decision on which ones to read. County librarians are usually able to advise on the titles in their reference departments. Viewing good auction sales armed with a good catalogue provides lessons and experience that can never be under-rated. Learn also of the antique dealers who specialize in your own interest and who can provide good advice; look for the kind of objects you are seeking, and they will also guarantee with a written description, whatever you may purchase from them.

Some people like to collect a particular class of object such as vesta cases or christening mugs. Some choose a period, occasionally as narrow as one particular year, others choose a style. Collecting the work of an individual silversmith or a family of silversmiths can also be fascinating. There are collectors who seek out objects related to their own profession, sport or craft. Opportunities for an active collector are almost limitless and the pleasure it brings does not wane with age. Whenever faced with the prospect of a purchase which they may consider just a little more than they can afford, collectors should ask themselves how long ago it was that they last saw an object of such quality, and how long it may be before they see another. If such a piece would form the centrepiece of a collection it might always be regretted later if such an opportunity was lost. On the other hand it would clearly be foolish to spend money on antiques that one could not afford.

During the first half of this century far too little attention was paid by most people to the makers of the silver they owned. Date and weight appears to have dictated the attitude of many collectors and most valuers. The tea and coffee pots were hung on scales and the weight read off. This was then multiplied by the market price per ounce, according to whether it was of the 18th or 19th century, and the value was arrived at. It should be remembered that the weight of precious metals is established on a special scale very different to the present day household scales. Value is always dependent upon the demand for any particular item; how many people there are wishing to buy in the market-place dominates all other factors. Of course weight is important, so is design and workmanship, and such extra details as engraved crests, coats of arms, and important inscriptions. Good, crisp hallmarks are also of major interest. A hallmark that has been worn or polished until it is unreadable will do the object no good at all.

Indeed, the fact that a hallmark reveals the silversmith to be a much favoured craftsman, can lift the value quite dramatically. Therefore, whenever cleaning silver always bear in mind that it is a soft metal, for during cleaning metal may be removed or made to change shape.

In other words, original detail should always be carefully retained; a high polish and blurred detail does no one any good.

A careful examination of the underside of a piece of silver, for which a good magnifying glass may well be helpful, will frequently reveal what is known as the scratch-weight, that is, the original weight of the object scratched into the base at the time of manufacture. This can be very important for it may sometimes reveal that alterations, have in some way taken place, or it can confirm that the condition is near mint. In other words, there is rather more to the understanding of silver than simply looking up a date in a pocket-book of hallmarks. Because many collectors do not expect silver to have been altered they seldom look for tell-tale signs. For example, someone in Victorian times may have inherited two fine, deep, square salt cellars from an 18th-century set. The new owner may then have asked his silversmith to add a cover to one of them in order to use it as a mustard pot. Such an object requires to be assayed, but few of them are. Whenever the purchase of a piece of silver is being considered, parts of which have been made separately – say the lid and handle of a coffee pot – both lid and handle should bear at least part of the main hallmarks found on the body of the piece. If not so marked or if a different mark is found on one of them, they are most unlikely to be original and this will adversely affect the value of the article.

From time to time a piece of silver will be discovered that contains what is known as a transposed hallmark, that is, the original hallmark has been removed and another substituted in its place. This type of fake was perhaps more frequently executed in Victorian times than it is now. An old mark from a fairly insignificant piece of silver might be clipped out and placed in a more important item. The tell-tale signs of such treatment are sometimes seen if the suspected mark is breathed upon when the outline of the substituted mark may become apparent. Today a genuine Georgian silver baluster-shape cup may be skilfully turned into a coffee pot after many additions have taken place. Passed on at a 'bargain' price in some minor auction or street market such pieces can create havoc for the unsuspecting purchaser.

Victorian silver posy holder with the original case

In the years immediately following World War II private buyers and dealers alike seemed intent upon removing all the crests and initials engraved on silver that came into their hands. The general feeling was that the centre of a silver dish or the side of a tea or coffee pot, etc., should be left clear for the initials of a new owner. Such thinking was entirely misguided; for one thing, the original engraving is part of the history of the piece, and for another too much silver is lost in the removal process. When looking at a silver teapot, for example, put both your thumbs over the area of the pot where you feel that such an engraved crest or initials may once have existed, and push. If any movement in the silver can be felt then the removal of a crest or similar device has taken place. This check is always worth doing with all crested and initialled pieces for they may well be second or third engravings. One can only advise against purchasing this category of object, as they have after all been weakened and are no longer in original condition. Value is very much affected, and even when temptingly offered cheaply it is usually worth waiting for something that has not been tampered with.

Many collectors dream of owning a fine silver tea service or a grand silver coffee pot of 1770, but objects of this calibre are today unquestionably costly. The word 'costly' is used advisedly for it indicates that an object has high value and is well worthy of it, whereas to use the word 'expensive' suggests that an object may be valued highly but is not worth it! All things that are made from precious metals will never be at the bottom end of the market, so it is almost inevitable that collectors will decide to gather around themselves carefully chosen small silver items that will not exert too great a strain upon the financial resources available. The popular enthusiasm for old silver

LEFT University of St Andrew's brooch, hallmarked Edinburgh 1877

as a hedge against inflation makes bargains hard to find, but for anyone prepared to learn and develop a sound knowledge of his chosen subject and to pursue it with tenacity, attractive purchases will inevitably be made. Before considering some specific area of collecting, the point must again be made that quality and condition is all-important. It is the eye of the connoisseur that requires to be nurtured; not the eye of the magpie attracted by everything that glitters.

Spoons

Spoons have a long history. It is said Moses made golden spoons for the Tabernacle, the Romans used silver spoons and they were familiar objects in the ancient Egypt civilizations. Early English silver spoons are very much collectors' pieces but they are rare and costly. Naturally, such spoons have also been copied, and outright fakes have been made particularly during the last century, but really good copies may well be worth including in any collection and are often very attractive; just so long as a 'copy' price is paid and not a 'genuine' one. Once again there is need to stress the importance of buying from dealers who specialize in the subject. The early spoons tend to be very plain in terms of the stem and the bowl, which is usually broad and shallow. Decoration comes in the form of knops which finish off the top of the stem on many spoons, although some are left plain. Puritan spoons, although somewhat bleak in appearance, are a pleasure to handle due to their robust weight. Acorn knops, seal tops, diamond point tops, are all found, together with occasional maidenhead spoons, so-called because they terminate in a female bust inspired by the Virgin Mary. All the spoons mentioned are rare but they will repay diligent study by the beginner for they demonstrate well the development of later spoon design, which is an obvious aid in dating. Another thing to note is how hallmarks are usually seen in the bowl or at the bottom of the stem in very early examples and then, as the centuries go by, they are struck increasingly higher on the stem until they virtually reach the top in modern times.

A design that most people will know of is the apostle spoon. They were made from the 14th century to the beginning of the 17th century. The Goldsmiths' Company have a complete set of thirteen, but individual examples are rare and it is this type of spoon that is most often copied in modern times. It was once a delightful custom for a child to be given an apostle spoon as a christening present. All the figures may be identified by the symbols they carry, which are as follows:— St Andrew with a saltire cross; St Bartholomew with a butcher's knife; St Jude (also known as Thaddeus) with a cross or club; St James the Less with a curved fuller's bat, for he was killed by a blow from Simeon the Fuller; St James the Greater with a staff, flask, and sometimes a scallop shell; St Mathius with an axe or halberd; St Matthew with a wallet or an axe; St Paul with a sword; St Peter with a key or a fish or both; St Philip with a staff or basket; St Thomas with a spear or builder's rule; St John with a cup, a branch or an eagle; St Simon Zelotes with a long saw, and, of course, Christ in Majesty.

Other popular spoon shapes are the *pied-de-biche*, also called a hind's-foot handle, the Trifid or lobe-ended spoon, Old English pattern, Rat tail spoons, so called because of the rib which tapers from the stem and reaches under the bowl. Onslow pattern takes its name from Arthur Onslow, 1691–1768, Speaker of the House of Commons. This elegant spoon with its curious curled end achieved considerable popularity and Onslow pattern spoons contemporary with Sir Arthur are rare though later examples will be found. The well-known Fiddle pattern appeared at the end of the 18th century, and from this evolved the King's pattern and Queen's pattern. Spoons with scroll engraving or 'picture' backs are also sought after.

Single teaspoons of variant designs and dates form excellent collections, and examples bearing what is known as bright-cut decoration have great charm. Bright-cutting is a form of engraving that reached its peak at the end of the 18th century, bevelled cutting producing a light reflecting sparkle to the spoon as one facet reflects another.

It is never advisable to buy spoons which have worn thin at the end of the bowl, unless of course the spoon is very rare, early or by a rare maker. Spoons that have worn in this way also tend to curl over slightly at the tip which can often be tested by carefully suspending the bowl from your finger nail.

Teaspoons developed with the rising popularity of tea drinking in England and a collection would look well together with a small group of well-chosen tea caddies and perhaps an example or two of the porcelain spoon trays that were once part of the 18th-century tea-services. In fact just a

Spoon end shapes: (*left to right*) Puritan (pied-de-biche); trifid; Old English; fiddle; King's pattern; fiddle pattern with thread and shell

A collection of table silver ranging in date from the early 19th century to the early 20th century. (*top left*) two pepper pots; three mustard pots; five salts; six tea spoons showing bright cutting; six caddy spoons (third from left shows Onslow pattern)

few of the host of objects associated with tea drinking and the ceremony it once was would make a fascinating assembly. One of the curiosities in silver that was very much part of the tea-making ceremony, was the mote spoon, or mote skimmer as it was also called. These spoons predate the silver tea strainer by a hundred years. Easily recognized, it was about the size of a teaspoon although the stem might be rather longer; the bowl was pierced with a pattern of round or shaped holes and was used for skimming off any floating tea leaves before handing the cups to the company. Another interesting feature of the mote spoon is its pointed, spear-like end. With this implement the holes leading from the body of the teapot to the spout could be kept clean and free of leaves so that the tea could be poured freely. Table and other large spoons are well worth collecting but well-marked heavy examples are likely to be costly although good buys are undoubtedly still to be found.

◪ CADDY SPOONS These beautiful little spoons have always been much admired and the interest in them and the enthusiasm for them has grown steadily over the years. There is even a Society of Caddy-Spoon Collectors. There are many designs to be found and a wide variety of materials were used for handles, particularly during the Victorian era. The early silver tea caddies had small domed lids which were used as tea measures, but as the caddy developed in size the need for a suitable spoon arose. Their hey-day was from the last quarter of the 18th century to the mid-19th century, but some excellent caddy spoons continued to be made beyond that date. Birmingham was renowned for its production of high-quality small silver and although other town marks will be seen, it is the Anchor mark of Birmingham that predominates among them.

Caddy spoons were made in a great variety of shapes: leaf, fish, shovel, scoop, shell, jockey cap, frying pan, and many more. Some were pressed, others cast; handles appear in an equal variety of shapes and materials – mother-of-pearl, bone and wood as well as silver are frequently seen. The jockey-cap shape is a special delight for most caddy-spoon collectors. Most genuine examples will carry the hallmark on the peak of the cap, which is used as a handle. Due to the popularity of this shape there have been many copies made, most of them from the backs of old silver watches. This usually results in the hallmark being located in the bowl of the spoon and such examples need examining with particular care.

Among the makers celebrated for their caddy spoons, as well as for much other fine silver are the Bateman family, including Hester, Peter, Anne, Jonathan and William Bateman, all of London. When Hester Bateman died in 1790, Peter Bateman formed a series of partnerships with his brother, wife and son: Peter and Jonathan Bateman 1790–91; Peter and Anne Bateman 1791–1805; Peter and William Bateman 1805–1815. William Bateman carried on the family business until *c*.1840. This was a fine family of silversmiths whose work is exceptionally well

TITLE PAGE Silver spoons, scoops and ladles together with skewers (often used as paper knives), a double-ended marrow scoop, and wood and whalebone-handled toddy ladles; the wooden-handled example has a Georgian silver coin set in the bowl. A fish slice and an ivory-handled cheese scoop are also illustrated

BELOW Ivory-handled silver trowel presented to J. Forbes Robertson on the laying of the commemoration stone of the Shakespeare Theatre, London, 1896

known and sought after and collected since World War II. The work of Hester Bateman is particularly admired in the United States and this has had the effect of increasing the value of her work against that of equally talented silversmiths of the same period. Her mark consists of her initials in script.

Other London makers include John Foligno, and Edward Farrell. Samuel Pemberton achieved a great reputation for the manufacture of small silver in Birmingham, as did Cocks and Bettridge. George Fenwick and William Cunningham, both of Edinburgh, are also names to look for but there were many fine silversmiths who produced at least a few caddy spoons.

SALT AND MUSTARD SPOONS These are also well worth collecting and can make a charming display in a small cabinet or even mounted as a wall decoration in a box frame. A profusion of designs again exist and many of the bowls of such spoons, and occasionally the entire spoon, will be in silver gilt. A thin wash of gold was found to be invaluable in protecting the silver from the harmful effects of salt. It is important to remember that salt must not be allowed to stand in silver salt cellars for any length of time or harmful effects on the silver will quickly result. Always wash silver items that have contained salt, following their removal from the table.

Scoops, ladles, servers, etc.

A most intriguing piece of small silver, the purpose of which continues to baffle many people, is the marrow scoop. This double-ended instrument consists in most cases of a different-sized scoop at each end. The object was the extraction of the marrow from cooked bones, highly regarded as a nutritious delicacy during the 18th century. Some spoons have their stems fashioned as marrow scoops but such examples are rare.

CHEESE SCOOPS continue to have a practical use and were first used for serving cheese at table in the late 18th century. They are not uncommon and handles are also seen in wood or ivory.

MEAT SKEWERS have been made and used from the early 18th century to the present day, although very few are now used for the purpose for which they were first designed. Silver skewers make ideal paper knives and the loss to the butler's pantry has been the gain of the executive desk. Most examples have well-struck hallmarks and their tops are both practical and attractive, being in the form of a shell or a ring.

TODDY LADLES may also be readily found. The bowls of such ladles are silver and are frequently set with a Georgian silver coin in the bottom of the bowl. As always, good hallmarks are important and some of the best ladles have whalebone handles, while others have turned wood handles.

FISH SLICES These attractive, broad-bladed servers were probably first used for serving whitebait in about 1770. Fish knives did not appear on the table until the 19th century. Many of the slices have pierced designs which allow liquids to strain through when in use and to be highly decorative when not. Most of the piercing on the early slices portray fish, but neo-classical shapes are by no means rare.

LADLES have always been popular with collectors. Used for soups and sauces they will enhance any table, but they look equally fine in a cabinet and are very satisfying objects to handle.

ASPARAGUS SERVERS are mostly of bow form, like sugar tongs, but often with pierced rectangular serving paddles. They are decorative and possess a curiosity interest and value. Often made by well-known silversmiths they are well worth seeking out. Some servers have a spring hinge rather than the bow shape mentioned earlier.

GRAPE SCISSORS or grape shears are most commonly found in either Sheffield plate or electroplate and should be by no means ignored. Silver examples are rare in comparison but with their vine-leaf and grape decoration they are very attractive. Most grape scissors are 19th century although 18th-century scissors do exist.

Carving sets, forks, fruit and bread knives, etc.

The satin or velvet lined fitted cases containing a carving knife, fork and steel of Victorian days are still readily obtainable. Few of these carving sets have silver handles but many of them have silver mounts or bolsters (the band of metal between handle and blade), most of which are hallmarked. The earliest table forks had only two prongs, then three, and it was not until the second quarter of the 18th century that they acquired four. Design and marking follow spoon patterns very closely. As with spoons worn examples are to be avoided unless a rare example is involved.

FRUIT KNIVES in the form of small clasp knives may be made entirely of silver or have mother-of-pearl handles. Most of those to be found are of the 19th century but well-hallmarked 18th-century knives may still be discovered in general antique shops. Silver bladed pea-knives are also well worth attention.

BREAD KNIVES with carved ivory or bone handles with silver mounts have now become somewhat scarce.

SUGAR TONGS Sugar tongs and sugar nippers hold a certain charm for most people, and they have the added advantage of being useful in the home today. Early sugar nippers have a scissor action as do some later examples, but these are rare. From 1750 onwards the bow-shaped tong is most used and shells form the most frequently used design for the grips. Superb collections of sugar tongs may be formed, as there is great variety of silver design, mainly in the patterns and techniques used in the decoration of the arms of the

Grape scissors (*centre right*); three sugar tongs; (*centre*) asparagus tongs; fruit knife (*front*); double-ended medicine spoon, and an ornamental dog table napkin ring form this group. The table napkin rings (*top left*) are the work of the renowned partnership of Omar Ramsden and Alwyn Carr, 1906

tongs. Victorian examples are still plentiful and may be bought accordingly.

◪ CARVER OR KNIFE RESTS Victorian rests, although often regarded as trivia in the past, have since resulted in several interesting collections being formed. In other words, everything that has been made with a practical and decorative purpose in mind should not be dismissed out of hand. Victorian knife rests may be found in materials besides silver, for example glass, plate, and ivory.

◪ CASTOR-OIL SPOONS Yet another splendid Victorian curiosity, these have a hollow stem down which the castor oil was poured in order to fill the reservoir at the 'bowl end' before the child opened its mouth and 'took the medicine'. Plated medicine spoons are not at all difficult to find.

◪ NAPKIN RINGS These do not receive the attention they deserve. Some are undoubtedly commonplace but many commemorative napkin rings were produced to celebrate anniversaries and such events as the launching of ships.

Wine labels

The first silver wine labels began to appear during the 1740s and they replaced the painted and hand-written labels used on bottles for so long. The wine label, or bottle ticket as it is sometimes called, brought a new elegance to bottles and decanters, the contents of which they named. The various shapes and patterns adopted by silver-smiths for the wine label amount to many hundreds of designs. Some labels take the form of rings which hang on the shoulders of the bottles, but by far the most popular shapes were the oblong and escutcheon shaped labels. To the collector of today it is by no means the shape and decoration of the label that is the sole attraction, for the names of the wines and cordials popular during the 18th and early 19th centuries form a facet of social history in themselves. Scores of names exist and lengthy research is often required in order to discover the nature of a particular alcoholic beverage.

The simple designs by lesser-known makers are by no means expensive, whereas there is great competition to obtain the fine pictorial labels of the 18th century. The production of wine labels began to fall following the Licensing Act of 1860 which stipulate the labelling of bottles sold to the public. A score of materials besides silver were used in label manufacture, some of the finest being in English or French enamel. Today some of the printed wine labels designed by celebrated artists for some of the great vintage clarets of France are themselves collectors' items. For the collector who is interested in the many antiques associated with wine, it is as well to be aware of the much larger metal or pottery 'bin' labels, which give such a touch of character to any wine-related collection.

Cases and boxes

◪ CARD CASES These are mostly 19th-century and made in many materials from ivory and papier mâché to tortoise-shell; it is the silver cases that are particularly desirable. Decoration is usually engined-turned, embossed or engraved, examples of the last being perhaps the most attractive of all. Fine cases were produced by the Birmingham makers; slim and elegant, they measure some four inches by three. Architectural subjects were highly favoured as decorative motifs, and often surrounded by generous floral scrolling. Abbotsford, home of Sir Walter Scott, Osborne House, home of the Victorian Royal Family, and the Crystal Palace, in company with many other famous buildings, all made their appearance on card cases. It is this class of card case that is most collected today.

VESTA BOXES If these small boxes had retained a plain rectangular shape with a rasp end, in order to contain and strike the tiny vesta matches so popular in the 19th and early 20th centuries, it is unlikely that they would ever have been deemed of importance. As ever, imaginative craftsmen were to produce a host of these silver match boxes in all manner of shapes including animals, fish and fruit. They were chased, engraved and engine-turned with great skill, and some are fitted with a ring for attachment to a watch chain. Collecting silver vesta boxes is a comparatively recent enthusiasm.

SNUFF AND TOBACCO BOXES Such boxes are undoubtedly desirable but the value of such items tends to be high. Many excellent books have been written on both types of box and it is suggested that interested collectors should turn to specialist dealers in snuff boxes. Unless today's collector of modest means is blessed with unusual luck, it is unlikely that a representative collection of snuff or tobacco boxes could now be formed without considerable financial outlay.

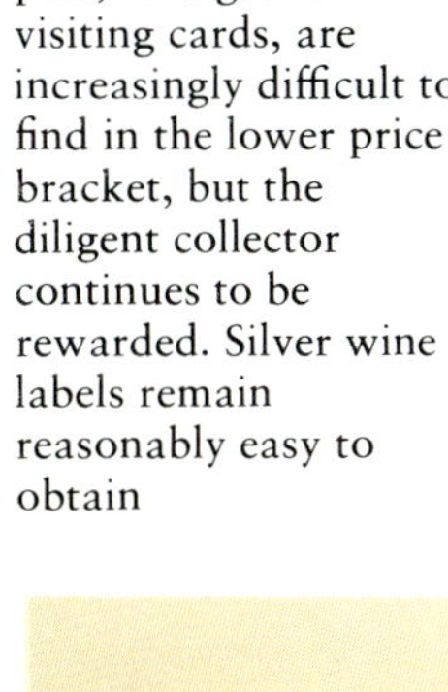
Silver boxes for snuff, pills, vinaigrette or visiting cards, are increasingly difficult to find in the lower price bracket, but the diligent collector continues to be rewarded. Silver wine labels remain reasonably easy to obtain

VINAIGRETTES These lovely little boxes were beautifully made to hold a small sponge primed with aromatic spices, and it was from this 'aromatic vinegar' that the boxes took their name. Superb vinaigrettes were made in silver and in gold and they have long been collected. Not surprisingly, considering their content, the interiors of the boxes are finished in silver gilt. Upon opening the vinaigrette, the outer lid exposes an interior pierced grill which holds the sponge in place. The grill is often extremely decorative with filigree or floral work and these boxes are the epitome of the silver box-makers' skill. The great Birmingham box-makers, Nathaniel Mills, Samuel Pemberton and Joseph Willmore, made many vinaigrettes but such pieces rarely come cheaply. They are seldom more than 4cm ($1\frac{1}{2}$in) in length, and frequently well under 2.5cm (1in). Embossed work, die stamping and engraving are regularly found among the decorative techniques employed on the vinaigrette. Occasionally a cowrie shell would be chosen to form the body of the box, or an Italian cameo might be employed instead of the more usual silver lid. Superb vinaigrettes were made in the Victorian period by such firms as Rawlings and Sumner and, later, Samson Mordan. Silver boxes in the form of books have always been collected and these are handsomely represented among vinaigrette shapes. Topographical views of London are highly prized, so too are boxes in the shape of shells. One of the finest 19th-century vinaigrettes handled by the author was a gold and enamel imperial crown set with gem stones, the initial letter of each stone spelling the name George.

As vinaigrette production moved into the Victorian era, so cast silver decoration increased on the edges of the boxes. It is at this period that vinaigrettes were frequently fitted with a silver ring in order that they might be fitted to a chain.

It would be an encyclopaedic task to list the vast array of silver that merits the collector's attention. The only advice that can be offered is to look, handle and learn. It is only by such methods that the discernment of quality and rarity becomes possible. All things of silver or mounted with that noble metal should be tested on the touchstone of individual taste: silver buttons, hat pins, photograph frames (particularly those with elements of Art Nouveau in their design), the silver-topped scent and pin boxes that once fitted superb Victorian dressing cases, paper knives, thimbles, button hooks, silver-framed pin cushions, silver bookmarkers and silver pen wipers. The list continues, as do the opportunities to exercise the gentle pleasure of having things about you in your home that will bring delight year in year out.

RIGHT A heart-shaped silver box and vesta case commemorating the third anniversary performance of *Charly's Aunt*, by Brandon Thomas, at the Globe Theatre, London, 21 December, 1895: *(lower right)* a vesta case commemorating the hundredth performance of Otho Stuart's production of *A Midsummer Night's Dream*, Adelphi Theatre, London, 1906

Paintings, prints and needlework

Pictures are executed in many mediums, oil, watercolours, and many different methods of engraving. Increasingly, it seems, the words 'genuine oil painting' is to be seen on the labels of pictures in shop windows; the words mean nothing more than that oil colours have been used to paint it. Many is the time picture experts have struggled to find some words of condolence after being called to examine some ghastly daub, only to be told by the pained and disappointed owner, 'but it's a genuine oil'.

People with a true love of pictures make the best collectors. They look at canvas after canvas and by experience build up an understanding of the painters in whom they are interested, and develop an eye for tone, subject and technique. Books and experts may provide information and some insight but in the final reckoning it is the individual's own response to a picture that matters. It is vital to be able to recognize quality in a work, and for this one looks for the sincerity of a painter and his skill and technique in translating this into his picture. Good drawing plays a vital role in painting, for how else are true scale and perspective to be achieved?

Because paintings and drawings form such a vast subject, it is important that a collector should decide from which artist or group of artists he wishes to collect, as well as choice of subject. Such a decision must always be a personal one, for the collector must really care about the pictures he intends to live with. A picture will not need to hang on your wall for long before you will know whether its future with you is to be old friend or

Still-life in oils by Stanley Wilson, 1871

passing acquaintance. Generally speaking it is the picture that rings with quality that finds an abiding place in the affections; the lesser works are usually recognized as such before they have been in your home two days.

Whether you are intending to buy at some minor auction, or have been asked to clear out the pictures from the attic of an old aunt, remember to look at the back of a picture as well as the front. You will be able to see if the canvas is an old one, and if it has been re-lined. Perhaps it has been painted on an old wooden panel, or a patent painting board of some kind. There may be old seals fixed to the panel or canvas that will enable its place in some previous private collection to be recognized. An old label may give information as to where it was once exhibited. A lot number may identify an important auction house through whose hands it has passed. A little spittle rubbed gently over what appears to be a signature will often open it up enough to be read. So many times these things are overlooked in favour of the gilding on the frame or the question of whether the brown in the foreground will go with the living-room carpet.

ABOVE An oil painting of Honfleur by James Wallace, 1905

RIGHT A fine watercolour portrait head of a Nubian by Elijah Walton, *c.* 1860

Any old picture of quality that is in a public auction will be looked at very carefully by experts, you can be sure, and it is unlikely that any bargains will be found in such company. Certainly masterpieces are discovered or rediscovered from time to time, but such occasions are rare, very rare.

Portraits, even very good ones, unless of some well-known personage, are likely to be purchased quite cheaply. Among the host of unknown portraits on the market it is virtually certain that the portrait of a woman will fetch more than that of a man, and that a man in a red or blue coat will be more expensive than one wearing brown. When you really feel you must own a painting, then that is usually the one to buy, provided it is within your budget. As the late R. O. Dunlop, RA, was to say on many occasions, 'When looking to buy a painting put your trust in God and keep your intuition bright.'

Any attractive 19th-century oil painting that has the touch of quality, be it landscape or still-life, is likely to be a good purchase, but unfortunately this is an area also frequented by the investor. Two painters whose work is worth looking for are Stanley Wilson, the still-life painter who was painting in London in the third quarter of the 19th century, and James Wallace who painted in England and France at the turn of the century; some of the latter's canvases show something of a post-impressionist quality. The early drawings of Eric Gill are decidedly underpriced, as are the drawings of James Guthrie, who founded the Pear Tree Press at the end of the 19th century. The paintings and drawings of Joseph Simpson are also ready for reappraisal; his sketches of personalities from the 1920s are frequently of a most dashing nature. The early palette-knife paintings by R. O. Dunlop are already being well pursued, but his drawings and watercolours have yet to receive the attention they deserve.

Britain is renowned for its watercolourists, and the famous names of Paul Sandby, John Varley, David Cox, Peter De Wint, and the rest, all fetch famous prices when their work comes on the market. But there are other members of the Varley family who also worked splendidly in watercolours, although their work fetches far less. During the Victorian period there were many amateur watercolourists of very considerable skill but few of whom signed their work. They painted views of houses, and land- and townscapes, and every now and then an antique shop or saleroom

FAR LEFT Pencil and wash drawing of the Market Cross, Chichester, Sussex, by Eric Gill, 1899

LEFT George Baxter print published 19 July 1856, showing a full-length portrait of Jenny Lind as Marie in *The Daughter of the Regiment*, by Gaetano Donizetti; a part in which she appeared in London at Her Majesty's Theatre in 1847

will yield a portfolio or album of such work that is worth its weight in gold.

The fashion for collecting etchings and engravings suffered a slump, yet there are now lively signs of revival. Quality remains quality; it is always fashion that is the fickle creature, and it is when an object of quality is out of fashion that it is time to buy.

Paintings by the 18th-century Smith brothers, William, George and John, could be purchased twenty-five years ago for well under a hundred pounds but now the value of some of their paintings has soared into several thousands of pounds. Their engravings and etchings, however, are frequently overlooked. A book containing fifty-three of their engravings was published by John Boydell in 1770, and this book in fine condition is now rare. Many of the books have been broken up and the engravings, mostly landscapes, dispersed. These are well worth acquiring should the opportunity occur.

David Lucas (1802–81) superbly engraved landscapes after John Constable. They are not at all uniform in size but they are delightful interpretations of the work of the great master of English landscape.

George Baxter (1804–67) was born at Lewes, the son of a printer. As a wood engraver he was working in London during his mid-twenties, intent on producing fine colour prints cheaply. Although colour printing had been carried out using wood blocks before, he employed a master plate followed by a series of wood blocks each applying oil-based colours. The register of his prints is remarkable and they have ever since been known as Baxter prints. In fine condition they possess a most beautiful bloom, but if exposed to strong light they fade very quickly. Courtney Lewis suggested in 1908 that collectors should ask themselves eight questions before buying a Baxter print. In abbreviated form they are as follows: **1** Has the print faded? **2** Is it in any way out of register? **3** Has it been printed from a worn plate? **4** Has it been cut? **5** Is its mount stamped and as issued? **6** If a book illustration, a design for sheet music or a needle case, is it complete? **7** Has it been printed with all its colours? **8** Has it been 'touched-up' by hand? All of the questions are equally relevant today. His subject matter ranged widely: *The Landing of Columbus, The Abolition of Slavery, Two Lovers standing under a Tree, Queen of Tahiti, The Bride, The Houses of Parliament, The Great Exhibition, Jenny Lind, Sir Robert Peel, Windsor Castle, The Holy Family*. Baxter's masterpiece was his *Coronation of Queen Victoria* print which includes two hundred portraits. All of Baxter's work is well worth obtaining when in good order. Between three and four hundred of his prints are obtainable. Baxter illustrated at least nineteen music covers.

Music covers

Pictorial music covers, such as those printed by Baxter, became popular in the early 19th century, and lithography was the main printing process used until the enthusiasm for chromolithography created the golden era (1860–1890) for sheet music covers. Sales were given a great boost with the development of music hall and other public entertainments which encouraged people to buy the music of the tunes and songs they heard, and repeat them at home on the parlour piano. Among the artists who designed covers were John Brandard, Alfred Concanen, and Edward Lear. The ballet music, the polkas and galops parade a stunning series of views, backdrops and battle-scenes. It would be true to say that in the space of a generation a whole social history of transport, dress, customs, and the conflicts of the Indian Mutiny and the Crimea, are all paraded on Victorian sheet music.

Prints

Prints should never be cut or cropped in any way. The indented outline of the edge of the plate carrying the engraving, that appears on many old prints, should never be interfered with. These lines are known as the 'plate mark'. The bottom left-hand corner of a print will often carry the name of the artist responsible for the original work. If the print was taken from a painting it will have the artist's name followed by the word 'pinxit'. If the original work was a drawing the legend would state '*delin*' or '*del*'. In the opposite corner the name of the engraver is usually shown followed by the word '*fecit*' or '*sculp*'.

The processes used in print production require careful study before a print can be picked up and immediately identified as, say, a line engraving or a soft etching. The main techniques are woodcuts, where the design to be printed is cut cross-grain, leaving the pattern in relief. Line engravings are cut into a copper plate leaving an intaglio design. Dots instead of lines were used for stipple engraving. Steel engravings enable lines to be cut much closer together than on the soft copper plate, and at times they produce a highly detailed and almost photographic effect. Steel engravings are now becoming increasingly looked for. They were very much part of the revolution in book design and illustration that advanced so rapidly in the 19th century. Many books illustrated with steel engravings are being broken up and the engravings sold as single prints. Many Victorians disliked steel engravings, feeling that they were too far removed from hard work. The steel plates themselves are now rare, as rust appears to have accounted for most of them, yet in their prime they were capable of producing many thousands of impressions without deterioration.

Mezzotints are created by working the entire surface of a copper plate which leaves it roughened. It is then prepared for printing with the aid of a scraper. Etching involves covering a plate with a coating of wax in which the design is drawn, then, by a series of dippings into an acid bath, the various lines and tones are eaten into the surface of the copper plate. Soft-ground etchings tend to produce the appearance of a pencil drawing, and many framed examples have been purchased in the belief that they were so.

Aquatint engraving gives the appearance of a watercolour. It is a rare and lovely form of illustration and the techniques of both mezzotint and etching are used. Lithography was invented in about 1796 and is a method whereby a surface print is taken from the surface of a prepared limestone. It is based on the antipathy of oil and water. A greasy crayon or ink is used to draw the design and the surface of the stone is made wet. Ink that will adhere to the design is rolled on to be followed

BELOW *The Great Exhibition Quadrille*, composed by Jullien, lithograph by John Brandard, 1851

BELOW RIGHT *The Cavalier's Pets*, steel engraving by J. Outrim after Sir Edwin Landseer, from *Landseer's Works*, published by Virtue, *c.* 1860

by the paper that will take the print. In chromolithography printing was done in individual colours from several lithographic stones or metal plates. Used in Britain from the early years of Queen Victoria's reign, new printing machines were to make colour printing available at a remarkably low cost. It should be remembered that many prints that are sold were never colour printes originally, but have been coloured later.

BARTOLOZZI was a Florentine who came to Britain in 1769 and became engraver to George III and a founder member of the Royal Academy. His engraved work is beautiful and yet at the moment it tends to be largely ignored. Fine Bartolozzi stipple engravings may be purchased very cheaply indeed, but it is unlikely that an engraver of such quality will remain out of fashion for too long. He engraved from the work of old masters, including Michelangelo; from his own period he favoured works of Sir Joshua Reynolds and W. Hamilton, RA. A series of prints called *Children at Play* are outstanding with their sense of gentle charm. Bartolozzi left England for Lisbon in 1802.

Maps

Among the earliest maps of Britain is the manuscript maps drawn and compiled by Matthew Paris of St Albans in about 1250. The product of years of research it was achieved by talking to travellers on the pilgrim road to Dover. Considering the period the work was done, the map is astonishing for there can be no mistaking the outline of Britain. Now it rests safely in the British Museum where it may be pored over by scholars after its years of use as a working tool.

There is a sense of romance surrounding all maps, and that is one of the reasons, no doubt,

FAR LEFT *Children at Play*, a sepia stipple engraving by Bartolozzi after Lady Diana Beauclerk

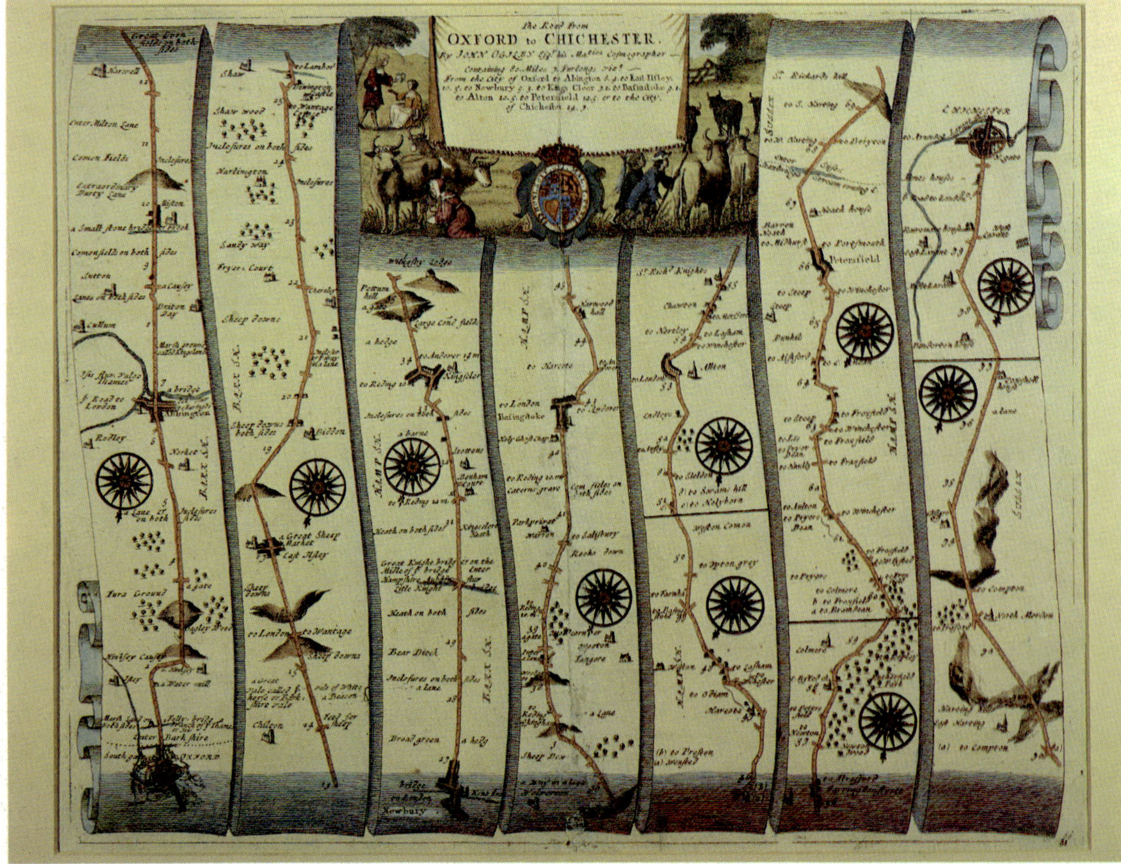

LEFT Strip map by John Ogilby showing the road from Oxford to Chichester, 1675

why so many people collect them. Looking at maps from the 15th century onwards and watching the world unfold is fascinating to say the least. Indeed, to see examples of the mapping of your own immediate geographical area is interesting enough and, again, there are many collectors who seek out all the different maps of their own county. The best-known early mapmakers are undoubtedly John Norden (1548–1626), John Speed (1552–1629) and Christopher Saxton (*c.* 1542–1606). It was Christopher Saxton who completed a fine atlas of the counties of England, and introduced a method of grading with the use of large and smaller italics to indicate the comparative importance of a town or other settlement.

Saxton's map of Cornwall, however, appears to be all ships and sea monsters, as though the map itself was something of an afterthought. The first mapmaker to mark the principal roads was John Norden.

Charles I hung maps on his walls and perhaps set the fashion for all of us. As always, fine early objects tend to be more difficult to find and thus more expensive, so most of us, I suspect, unless we settle for a copy, will look for something rather later in date which in its own way will be equally interesting and perhaps more relevant to the landscape we know.

John Ogilvy (1600–76) was born in Edinburgh, and it was he who invented the use of strip roadmaps. It was a superb achievement that unfolded the road ahead, noting the miles and pointing out landmarks to the traveller. Later editions of the Ogilvy road maps are not too difficult to find.

Maps of Australia and North America change constantly through the 19th century. In Britain towns were expanding with the industrial revolution and railways cut new routes across the countryside. These later maps may often be obtained very cheaply. If the idea of collecting maps appeals to you, then the best advice would be to seek out the leading map dealers where stocks are truly comprehensive.

Old maps were either coloured or left plain, although most of the plain maps were coloured at a later date. The fashion for colour emanated from the Netherlands where map colouring was virtually a natural progression from illuminating manuscripts in earlier centuries. Most of the paper used in those days was well watermarked and the presence of a watermark can help to date an unusual map, but whether such a mark is present or not has no influence on the value of a map. Another feature to look for is the mesh effect caused by the wire trays in which the hand-produced paper was dried. This network of lines is easily seen when a map is held to the light.

Berlin woolwork

In a painting by Holman Hunt, *The Awakening Conscience*, work may be seen in progress on a piece of Berlin woolwork. Fine coloured worsted wools taken from the backs of merino sheep of Saxony, and dyed in Berlin was used. Early in the 19th century the owner of a Berlin print shop devised a series of squared patterns, each square representing a stitch that could be copied on to canvas squared in the same manner, using the brilliantly coloured Berlin wools in either tent or cross stitch. The first working of these patterns was carried out by the Berlin print-seller's wife, who proved the simplicity of the method. The patterns sold widely and for the Victorian lady the Berlin embroideries became a passion. They were used for upholstery and chair covers, and very soon biblical and other scenes were embroidered for framing, often in firescreens. Cushion covers, carpets and rugs and even 'texts' were all worked in a similar manner.

Wool and silks began to be used together and glass beads also became fashionable in embroidery. Historical and literary scenes were translated into embroidery, as were works of Sir Edwin Landseer, stags in particular. Among the portraits of the Royal Family carried out in Berlin woolwork that of the Prince of Wales in Highland costume was the most popular. When some of these portrait designs were used to upholster footstools there were those who were quick to point out that by so doing the heir to the throne was being trodden under foot. Another favourite subject was Moses in the bullrushes. Such embroideries created a brave splash of colour in the Victorian household. Berlin woolwork has survived in considerable quantity, particularly the framed pieces. These are well worth collecting, especially the smaller embroideries with birds, fruit and flowers, the narrative firescreen panels, and all pieces of good beaded

RIGHT A coloured paper pattern squared as a guide for stitching. These tapestries, when finished, are known as Berlin woolwork

Woolwork portrait of a steam frigate in its original maple frame, *c.* 1860

work that is in good order. Some of the small circular footstools that are so frequently seen are excellent examples of this technique.

Woolwork pictures

Soldiers once had a tradition of working representations of the regimental badges in wool embroidery, and many thousands of handkerchiefs and table covers bearing such badges as souvenirs have been commercially produced. The troops probably obtained the idea from the Royal Navy while they were being carried to wars and outposts overseas.

It is the wool portraits of ships, worked while sailors were off-watch, that are now claiming the keen attention of collectors as well as naval historians. Such pictures, most of which possess a most appealing naïve charm, enjoyed great popularity between 1850 and 1880 and this thirty year period is undoubtedly their golden age.

The pictures were made from sailcloth stretched on a simple wooden frame and the outline of the vessel was then sketched in. Wool was the most usual material for stitching but cotton, linen and (with care) silk were also used. Silk might be employed for sails, and button thread for rigging. Examples are occasionally seen with sails or waves filled out by the use of cuttle-shell under the wool.

The best of these ship pictures pay considerable attention to detail often making it possible to date the vessels with some accuracy. Dates are sometimes worked into the pictures, as are the names of ships. As always it is the fine specimens that should be sought by collectors. Late examples are somewhat roughly embroidered and lack the feeling of care and pride that pervades the better wool pictures. Thankfully, very few copies of these pictures have been made and they are, in fact, very difficult to fake, the ageing of the materials used proving the main stumbling block. The original frames found on wool pictures tend to be in maple wood with a narrow gilt mount.

Great care needs to be taken if it becomes necessary to remove an embroidery from its frame. Rough handling may cause rigging to become loose and dust is best removed by a small bellows rather than the application of a cleaning liquid which might seriously affect the nature and quality of the picture.

Many suggestions have been put forward as to the reason for sailors taking up this form of activity in the mid-19th century. Captain Steven Banks, RN (Rtd.) believes they may have been inspired by the Chinese embroideries sold to sailors when Far Eastern ports were opened up to the West in the early 1840s. During World War I wounded sailors and soldiers were often given, while recuperating, perforated cards with needles and wool for sewing representations of Allied

Silk-worked embroidery containing a contemporary photograph of a soldier, World War I

flags, etc. Larger embroideries were also made, sometimes forming the surround to a photograph portrait of a soldier or sailor. While these cannot be compared with the quality of the wool embroidered ship portraits they have, sixty years on, acquired an interest of their own.

Needlework samplers

Samplers date from the early 16th century. The first mention of the word occurs in 1502 in an inventory of Queen Elizabeth of York, '. . . linny cloth for a sampler for the Quene . . .'. French knots, Italian cross stitch, arrow heads, back, buttonhole and chain stitches all appear together with many more on the early samplers. The shape of the older samplers was also different for they were long and narrow, and 15 x 76cm (6 x 30in) was not unusual. Above all they were carefully stitched as a record, a work of reference in respect of patterns, at a time when pattern books were very rare. It was also a period when the accomplished needle-woman was held in very high esteem. Most of these long samplers were divided into separate bands of stitches and patterns, and were regarded as very personal objects, signed by the women who created them and usually having the dates that they were worked.

One of the finest accounts of the early use of samplers appears in a story by Barnabe Riche published in 1581. It describes how the wife of a wealthy man might spend her time. 'Now, when she had dined, then she might go seke out her examplers, and to peruse which worke would doe beste in a ruffe, whiche in a gorget, whiche in a sleeve, whiche in a quaife, whiche in a caul, whiche in a handcarcheef, what lace would doe beste to edge it, what seame, what stitche, what cutte, what garde. And to sit her doune and take it forthe by little and little, and thus with her nedle to passe the after noone with devising of thinges for her own wearyng.' Our use of the word sampler derives from the word 'exampler' as used in the above quotation. Great country houses gathered samplers as they would books for a library. They were much treasured and were not infrequently made the subject of bequests.

Needlework sampler by Elisabeth Kincardine, 1855

It was towards the middle of the 18th century that samplers increasingly began to take on the square appearance most often associated with the samplers we see today. The sense of a practical guide and pattern book began to diminish and the sampler became more of a picture for framing and displaying upon the wall. Floral borders enclosed biblical texts, houses, trees, animals, birds, windmills, gardens, farmyards, and the occasional silk worked map showing the counties of England. Many of the later samplers were the work of children, most of them aged between seven and twelve years. The making of samplers was an activity pursued in many village schools. A fine series of these is to be seen at Sudeley Castle, Winchcombe, Gloucestershire. Elizabeth Clements of the Charity School ends her sampler with the thankful lines: . . .

> This I have done, I thank my God,
> Without correction of the rod.

Or, as a seven-year-old girl stitched in 1813: 'Not Land but Learning, makes a man complete, Not Birth but Breeding makes him Great, Not Wealth but Wisdom does adorn his State, Virtue not Honor makes him fortunate. Learning, Breeding, Wisdom, Get these Three, Then Wealth and Honor Will attend on thee.'

Stevengraphs, postcards and cards

Stevengraphs

This is the name given to silk-woven pictures produced by Thomas Stevens of Coventry. Their patterns are elaborate and full of detail, the colours well chosen and strong. Most of these little pictures have a standard size of 15cm (6in) by 5cm (2in), but variations do exist. Originally they used named mounts which could be purchased for a shilling (5p) unframed, while for 2/6d (25p) they were obtainable in gilded 'Oxford' frames. Hundreds of patterns and variations were sold during a golden period of popularity that lasted some thirty years. Stevens had first produced silk-woven bookmarkers as early as 1862, but it was at the York Exhibition which opened on 7 May 1879, and continued until the end of October that year, that the Stevengraph was launched in great style. Visitors to the exhibition were able to watch Stevens' great machines, developed from the earlier Jacquard loom invented by Joseph Jacquard, create the first two Stevengraph pictures which made perfect souvenirs to carry home from the exhibition.

The two first subjects were brilliantly chosen. One was of the *London and York* stage-coach well laden and drawn by a spanking team of four horses. On the mount below the picture are the words: 'From the "Black Swan" Holborn, London, To the "Black Swan" Coney Street York'. It was a coach service that had started running in 1706, and the picture clearly captured the imagination of a wide section of the public. The picture was soon to be revised with the title *The Good Old Days*, but it is not to be confused with the original examples, the mounts of which, woven at the York Exhibition, carry a legend to that effect in the bottom left-hand corner.

The second of the two pictures has the title *Stephenson's 'Triumph' Sixty Miles an Hour*. The train, the *Lord Howe*, is shown pulling two carriages and the legend on the mount below the picture states 'The first train ran on September 27th, 1825. From Stockton to Darlington.' Again, the bottom left-hand corner contains the words, 'Woven in the York Exhibition 1879'. As with the previous picture, Stephenson's 'Triumph' was revised under the title *The Present Time*.

A stream of silk pictures began to pour from the many looms of Thomas Stevens. His beautiful bookmarkers had made him known to the public over many years and goodwill towards him could hardly have been greater when his new lines were introduced. The pictures spanned views, portraits, sporting and historical subjects opening up a magnificent panorama for the collector.

▨ LANDSCAPE VIEWS include Balmoral Castle, Clifton Suspension Bridge, Conway Castle and Bridge, Coventry, The Crystal Palace, The Edinburgh International Exhibition of 1886, The Forth Bridge, The Mersey Tunnel Railway (showing a train going through the tunnel and ships sailing above), The Tower of London, Houses of Parliament, Windsor Castle, and God Speed the Plough.

▨ SPORTING SCENES include an Oxford *v.* Cambridge Boat Race, cricket, hare-coursing, fox-hunting, Iroquis winner of the 1881 Derby with Fred Archer up, Victorian penny-farthing cycle racing, bull-fighting, rugby, lawn tennis.

The double silk Stevengraph woven at the York Exhibition of 1879

A view of an American baseball match in progress, *c.* 1880. It is among the rare silks of Thomas Stevens

HISTORICAL SCENES include the lifeboat rescue by Grace Darling, fire-engines, the death of Nelson (showing Admiral Lord Nelson on deck, rather than in the cockpit of *Victory* where he died), Dick Turpin, trains, portraits of battleships, Lady Godiva, Wellington and Blücher, Radetsky and King Victor Emmanuel.

AMERICAN INTEREST includes *Columbus leaving Spain*, *The First Innings* (baseball match *c.* 1880), *The Home Stretch* (Trotting Match), *Landing of Columbus* (this forms a pair with *Columbus Leaving Spain*) and they were first issued at the Chicago World's Columbian Exposition of 1893), *Niagara*, *Signing of the Declaration of Independence* 4 *July* 1776 (early examples have the wording 'Woven in pure silk at the World's Columbian Exposition, Chicago, 1893').

PORTRAITS include Queen Victoria, Lord Beaconsfield, Gladstone, Robert Burns, Buffalo Bill, John L. Sullivan, George Washington, Shakespeare, Henry Morton Stanley, Dr W. G. Grace, the Tsar and Tsarina of Russia, Lord Roberts, Lord Kitchener, Lt.-Col. Baden-Powell, King Edward VII, King George V and Queen Mary, and numerous sporting personalities.

As well as the attraction to be found in individual pictures, the variations in lettering, borders, colours, and the versions of designs made over a period of years are of intense interest and importance in terms of dating, rarity and value. Some silk pictures were also produced in postcard form. Stevens' bookmarkers are still readily obtained and fine collections may still be formed.

Two Stevengraphs flanking a silk-woven portrait of Lord Randolph Churchill by W. H. Grant of Coventry

The grandest ribbon of all was the great sash woven for the Ancient Order of Foresters by Thomas Stevens, the design of which was registered in 1873. In August of that year, Francis Bennock, reviewing for the *Journal of the Royal Society of Arts*, turned his attention to the silk goods on show at the 1873 Exhibition.

'. . . Mr Stevens evidently possesses a restless spirit, not easily subdued, and if the tide threatens to leave him for a time, he digs out a new channel for himself, and thus he has created a trade peculiarly his own. I have taken unusual interest in his productions, not only in the goods, but in the looms producing them, and I find that to make a "Forester's scarf" as exhibited, 229cm (7 ft) long and 15.9cm ($6\frac{1}{4}$in) wide, requires the use of 16,000 perforated cards to make the figure, which is 38cm (15in) long, and for the plain part 14,000 cards, making a total of 30,000 cards. The number of threads in the warp of each scarf is 1,800, and there are fifteen different colours in the shutes; these figures are multiplied by the number of pieces being made at once; so that if ten pieces were making, 18,000 threads of warp would be in the loom. Hence the involved, and, to the untrained eye, the inextricable confusion of threads, as shown in the harness of the loom.

'It requires about six months to fit up such a loom, and when it and the cards are all ready, it occupies a month to obtain one complete pattern. Eight pieces are made at once in the loom now at work, and with ten hours' labour a good hand will make the length of one scarf each day. The cost of the loom, the draft or design, the cards, and the value of the silk in the loom, would make a total value of £500.'

Anyone with a memory of the antique market during the early part of the war period will recall that values of objects made after 1850 were depressed, to say the very least. A good quality Victorian chiffonier might then have been purchased at auction for under £1, silver of the period was ridiculously cheap, although a few sages in the trade declared from time to time that, 'A £10 piece of Victorian silver bought now, could be a great investment for the future.'

It was many years before Stevengraphs became

popular and during the summer months of 1963 a large exhibition of Stevengraphs opened in the London Gallery of Messrs Frank T. Sabin. Some of the silk pictures were priced as high as £12! The revival of interest had begun, and the pace increased as the sixties progressed. A London firm of auctioneers, Messrs Knight, Frank, and Rutley, began to feature them in their catalogues and even created the first specialist sales. The results were gratifying and a broadly based market was established.

The publication in 1971 of a definitive reference book by Mr Geoffrey A. Godden, *Stevengraphs*, subtitled *and other Victorian silk pictures* is a work of major importance to all enthusiasts. In the preface to this fine work Mr Godden states, '. . . if anyone had purchased in 1902 the 66 subjects then available, the total expenditure would have been only £2-9s-6d (£2.47½). Today (1971), these same Stevengraphs would cost over £3,000!'

When purchasing silk-woven pictures the necessity of obtaining pictures in good condition should be kept well in mind. They should be clean, undamaged and the colours strong. Many Stevengraphs are seen that have been remounted. This very much affects their value and unless very rare should not be considered. A cracked mount will also affect value and repaired items are best left well alone as near an original state as possible should be the byword of the collector. Far too many of the silk-woven bookmarkers are found today minus their tassels and with the threads of texts and patterns considerably disturbed, which is usually due to them having been badly folded and creased. Silks need to be kept flat and well away from strong sunlight and damp.

Before going on to list some of the other important manufacturers of silk-woven pictures in Britain, due acknowledgement requires to be made to the man who first made such pictures a possibility – Joseph M. Jacquard. The earliest silk-woven pictures were manufactured in France on the draw looms employed at Lyon during the last thirty years of the 18th century. From 1839 onwards the Jacquard loom, with its many advantages over the earlier looms, was being used. It controlled the number and order of warp threads raised for a simple pass on the weft. Jacquard was born in 1752 at Lyon where the main local industry was silk weaving, and while working in the local mills he developed his ideas for an improved loom. When he was sixty years old there were at least ten thousand of his looms working in France. Napoleon granted Jacquard a state pension, and following his death in 1834 a statue was erected in his honour at Lyon.

On the Thomas Stevens' machines the designs were fed on to the Jacquard loom by a series of punched cards and the holes in the cards found the pattern by selecting the warp and weft threads and the colours required; in other words, an early computer technique.

There were many continental manufacturers of silk pictures and these are well worthy of further study, but here we will concern ourselves only with the British manufacturers. John Ratliff & Son were Coventry manufacturers of ribbons, who wove patterned and lettered ribbons during the 1860s. John Caldicott of Coventry was the first manufacturer to register the design of a bookmarker ribbon. This was early in 1862, a few months before Stevens was registering his. Caldicotts bookmarkers included the head of Christ with the words 'I am the Light of the World'. His ribbon designs included portrait heads of the Madonna, Prince Albert, Shakespeare, and a number of others. Henry Slingby of Coventry wove various sash and scarf ribbons and is known for his silk badge to commemorate the 85th anniversary of the American Declaration Of Independence. Mulloney & Johnson of Coventry were convicted of infringing one of Thomas Stevens' registered designs, but they went on to produce the first anniversary ribbons to mark the three-hundredth birthday of William Shakespeare. Welch & Lenton of Coventry were well known for their bookmarkers and also produced silk-centred valentines and Christmas cards. At the York Exhibition of 1879 they also had a loom on display and produced the official Exhibition bookmarkers.

Another famous name among the Coventry weavers is that of J.J. Cash who continues to flourish in the city today. Much of their output in the 19th century was concerned with the supplying of name tapes, but they also made ribbons, badges and initial letters, as well as white and coloured frillings; they did, however, produce occasional silk-woven prints. Messrs. Dalton & Barton produced some excellent silk pictures and these are usually dated. They depicted various members of the Royal Family, an outstanding example being the portrait of H.R.H. Prince Alfred Ernest Albert, with the title *England's Royal Sailor*. The young prince with telescope under his arm is an excellent example of precise weaving.

Collecting postcards

The first commercial postcards appeared in Austria in 1869, just a matter of months before the Franco-Prussian War broke out in 1870. The cards were prepaid at a cheap rate and provided space for a brief message. The idea had come originally from Dr Heinrich von Stephan, a German statesman who, at a postal conference in 1865, suggested they might prove to be of military use in terms of communication. Although the Austrian Post Office was to take up the idea, Germany was quick to follow suit and introduced views and colour printing. The Chicago World Fair of 1893 launched the sale of postcards in America, although it was several years before they were generally available. In Britain, however,

ABOVE Silk birthday bookmarker by Thomas Stevens

HALF-TITLE Thomas Stevens bookmarker, the design of which was registered 5 May 1871

the publication of postcards commercially did not occur until 1894, due to Post Office rules. The early postcards had to conform at first to the size of the Post Office cards, but the first few years of the 20th century saw the establishment both of a highly profitable business in postcards and of such great card firms as Valentine's of Dundee, and Raphael Tuck. Another celebrated early firm specializing in early photographic views was Messrs F. Frith of Reigate. Many of the coloured postcards by British firms were printed in Germany, a country that for years was the centre of the postcard market.

In Britain artists from *Punch* brought out comic postcards, and the humourous and saucy postcard has always maintained an important position in the market. The works of such artists as Phil May, Lance Thackeray, and later Donald McGill were about to become national institutions. When a plaque was unveiled in 1979 to mark the London birthplace of McGill a pair of Queen Victoria's white drawers was used as the curtain that was lowered at the ceremony. Phil May (1864–1903) was a Yorkshireman with a particular liking for London. His drawings of working-class cockney children are superb and he captured and handled the social life and humour of the nineties with great skill. He also worked for three years in Australia.

Louis Wain (1860–1939) will always be remembered for his anthropomorphic cats for which he too became noted in the nineties. His postcards, Christmas cards and original drawings are now much in demand. G. E. Studdy introduced the comic dog Bonzo to a delighted postcard audience, and Mabel Lucie Attwell became a household name with her sentimental, but charming and often very funny drawings of plump babies and toddlers. In 1979, the centenary of Mabel Lucie Attwell's birth, an exhibition of her work showed the full range and quality of her insight and drawing. Her postcards have begun to rise considerably in value and are likely to become increasingly scarce in the next few years as more collectors take her toddlers to heart, with their sense of nostalgia. The search for Valentine's 'Attwell' series will bring much pleasure.

Postcards are to be found to suit all tastes and enthusiasms. The cards of Mabel Lucy Attwell *(bottom left)*, are increasingly sought after items

During the late Victorian and the Edwardian periods, a Scots cartoonist calling himself Cynicus, achieved a reputation for his biting social and political cartoon comments. He published his work through books and postcards from his own 'Cynicus Publishing Company Ltd' at Trayport in Fife. As long ago as 1942 the great cartoonist David Low was pointing out the importance of Cynicus – in his words, 'the authentic latter-eighteenth-century spirit'. It is only recently, however, that the excellent postcards by Cynicus have begun to be collected. His social satire, often very light hearted, was quick to see the humour in human situations common to us all.

The Raphael Tuck & Sons' 'Oilette' cards are an important series. One of their major artists was Harry Payne who did fine military studies and also superb paintings that provide us with a glimpse into rural life in the early years of the century.

Some of the most attractive cards to be published during the First World War, and later, are those taken from original watercolour views. The name perhaps most frequently observed on these cards is that of A.R. Quinton who seems to have supplied a large number of his watercolours to the firm of J. Salmon of Sevenoaks. There were, however, many other publishers and watercolourists of this period who, with Quinton, well deserve attention.

Among the millions of photographic postcards there is much opportunity for the discriminating collector. There is the obvious choice of bringing together a photographic postcard record of the place in which we live. The change that has been wrought between, say, 1910 and the present day in our local high street, is usually astonishing. These cards are historically important and may be by such firms as Valentine or Frith. Even more interesting are cards that portray a particular shop, its goods, window display, and packaging, and perhaps the proprietor and his staff as well. Many cards provide information on fashion, means of transport, monuments or buildings that have since been destroyed, or countryside that now lies under concrete. In many cases it was the local photographer at the turn of the century who captured events on his glass plate negative that would otherwise not have been recorded at all. The limited issue of real photographs as postcards of, perhaps, an early horse fair, might well prove to be the only known record. Photographs and postcards are now well recognized as major historical documents. There is much else that needs to be considered. What about philately and postal history? The stamp or postmark or both may be of special interest. The sender or the recipient of an old postcard might be of particular note; a famous scientist, politician, writer or artist. Sometimes a postcard may be interesting simply because of its humorous, ambiguous, or cryptic message.

Novelty postcards that provide a joined strip of a dozen local seaside views when a tab is pulled are not uncommon, but they are far more prone to damage than the standard postcard. Others were described as puzzle pictures, setting the task of discovering the features of some well-known personality. In 1914 a postcard appeared depicting a seaplane; the puzzle part of it came in the simple instructions, 'Find Winston Churchill'. Other cards revealed extra or hidden detail when held to the light, and there are cards that squeak when pressed.

Continental postcards, particularly those in the Art Nouveau style, are now much in demand. The Viennese firm of M. Monk issued many fine cards of this type. Alphonse Mucha designed numerous series of postcards which are now rare and valuable. G. Mouton and Xavier Jagar in Paris concentrated on supplying the rest of Europe with their postcards of seductive women in provocative poses.

▨ SILK-WOVEN POSTCARDS The silk-picture postcards of Thomas Stevens, W.H. Grant, and others, already mentioned under Stevengraphs, continue to be a rich mine for the prospecting collector. They are to be obtained far more cheaply than Stevengraphs and are easily maintained in modern albums for reference and pleasure. They take the form of the basic postcard but instead of bearing a photographic or painted scene, a silk-woven picture has been 'laid in'. Although intended for use through the posts very few are found stamped and franked although their sale was considerable. A card of this type, therefore, having gone through the post and being in good condition should be prized.

All the silk-woven British postcards belong to the present century, but it is very likely that their production was inspired by the introduction of silk cards on the Continent during the 1890s. W.H. Grant was certainly a leader in the field, but some of the early Stevens' postcards were sold by R.T. Morgan & Co. of London as though the cards were their own product, a fact borne out by their publicity and advertisements at the time. The most successful early silk-woven postcards contained a view of the Crystal Palace.

As usual Thomas Stevens spread his choice of subjects widely: Tower Bridge, Peeping Tom, Ann Hathaway's Cottage, Monarch of the Glen, St Paul's, W.G. Grace and many others. Some of these postcard subjects were simply scaled down versions of the larger Stevengraphs. A long series of cards depicting great passenger liners was issued including such famous vessels as the R.M.S. *Aquitania*, the *Carmania, Lusitania, Mauretania*, and the ill-fated *Titanic*. Cards of the *Titanic* are obviously rare.

The firm of W.H. Grant & Co. produced considerable numbers of silk-woven cards and more subjects than Thomas Stevens. Grant, like Stevens, realized that the tourist was the most likely purchaser of such postcards as souvenirs, and he too wove the almost obligatory representations of such places as Shakespeare's birthplace and Ann Hathaway's cottage.

Valentines

The printed and embossed valentine cards in the form we recognize them today are very much the product of the 19th century. Valentines in the form of decorated love letters, however, were well known in the 18th century, particularly in Germany. The valentine takes its name from a bishop, Valentinus, who was martyred by the Romans on the eve of Lupercalia, 14 February, and became the patron saint of all lovers. The 18th-century valentine is a rarity but the commercial valentine – and there could hardly be a more typical example of Victorian sentiment – is well worth collecting. Paper valentines with engraved or lithographic outlines were hand coloured and these soon found favour, so much so that fine embossed paper and lace paper were soon enlisted to form the framing and backgrounds for decorative ribbons, pressed flowers, model hearts and silk-covered scent satchets. Cupid signed banknotes issued by the Lovers' Banking Company at Love Lane, and promising to pay on demand the entire love of the sender.

The firm recognizable for the first of the exotic valentines was that of H. Dobbs, 'Ornamental Stationer' to the Royal Family. There were cards with little doors opening to reveal a marriage service taking place within; others in which the pulling of a tape or string caused part of a cut-paper design to pull out into a three-dimensional basket of flowers or bird cage. In 1875 it was estimated that some 10,000 people were employed in the valentine trade. The heyday of the valentine was the twenty years from 1840 to 1860. After that period the manufacturers began thinking in terms of mass production but such methods were well justified in view of Britain's rapidly growing population.

The level of extravagance the valentine was to reach is astonishing. Velvet, feathers, wax flowers, cork, looking glasses, even paste jewellery were used to create a sense of deep plush opulence heavy with sentiment. As the century moved on the character of valentines began to change yet again. The nesting birds, cupids, and idyllic cottages had not lost favour, but the cloak of anonymity given the sender by the penny post began to

RIGHT Walter Crane celebrated for his illustrated books for children was also a highly successful designer of valentine and other greeting cards

FAR RIGHT A Victorian valentine by H. Dobbs, one of the leading early card designers

be realized. Cards appeared that insulted the recipient's physical appearance. The slightly improper cards emerged. When a tag was pulled on a card depicting a lovely young crinolined lady she would raise her skirt to provide a glimpse of her bloomers!

The bright colours of chromolithography were increasingly employed and the work of leading artists and designers began to be employed in the card trade. Marcus Ward & Company had Thomas Crane as director of their design department. More of their cards became dual purpose and might be used as either valentines or Christmas cards. Walter Crane, Thomas's brother, designed a number of these cards and they are of high quality. To the valentine collector it is important to know the manufacturer and date of the valentines that he or she is fortunate to come across. Such names are often found printed or embossed within the design of the card. Recognition of styles and techniques may well lead to correct attribution concerning unsigned specimens. Dating may well be assisted by a dated watermark in the paper, although it is obvious that the date of the paper could be considerably earlier than the date when the paper valentine was manufactured. Among the main valentine makers and designers are the following: John Leighton, using the pen name Luke Limner (mentioned further on page 45); George Corbould; The Cruikshank brothers; Joseph Mansell; Joseph Addenbrooke; T.H. Burke; De La Rue; H. Dobbs (later Dobbs & Company); George Kershaw; George Meek; John Windsor.

Fine examples of valentines are to be found from time to time safely preserved in family scrapbooks. The valentines of the painter Joseph Mansell (1803–1874), may be considered a rarity. He was also well known as a licensee of the George Baxter process of printing in oil colours.

VALENTINES BY THOMAS STEVENS OF COVENTRY In 1862 Thomas Stevens advertised for the first time: 'VALENTINES, beautifully woven in silk, from 2/6 (25p) to 12/- (60p).' The valentines mentioned may well have been no more than bookmarker ribbons at this date, woven with suitable verses and designs.

Valentine cards with a Stevens' silk-woven panel set in a firmly cut paper surround on a card mount are now rare, but there is no doubting their attractive quality, as the *County Herald* of 31 January 1868 was quick to point out:

'By the aid of Cupid and beautifully cut paper and ribbon, Mr Stevens has turned out some very tasty things in this department which any lady may be glad to possess as works of art, irrespective of the love they are intended to symbolize, and we are glad to hear that they have commanded the large sale they deserve.'

Never a man to stand still in terms of production, Stevens was again making the impact of his firm felt by introducing a new range of novelties that included: 'Valentines containing silk embroidered jewellery, neck ribbons, Bows for the Hair, etc; 12/- (60p) to £5 per dozen.'

Christmas cards

The first Christmas card made its appearance in 1843 when Henry Cole asked J.C. Horsley, RA, to design a Christmas greeting for his friends. Horsley devised a card divided into three parts, the two side panels representing 'Feeding the hungry' and 'Clothing the naked', and the centre panel portraying a family group happily drinking the toast which was printed underneath, 'A merry Christmas and a happy New Year to you'. About a thousand of these cards were produced using a lithographic process, after which they were hand coloured. Jobbits of Warwick Place, Holborn, were the printers, and only a score of these cards appear to have survived. Messrs De La Rue reprinted this card in chromolithography in 1881.

Henry Cole took a great personal interest in design and he won a Society of Arts prize for his simple design of a tea-set made by Mintons. He used the pseudonym Felix Summerly in many of his enterprises and the Art Union magazine announced in their issue for June 1847, that: '"Felix Summerly" has introduced several of the most eminent British artists to make designs for British manufacturers – a course we have strongly advocated for years, and ernestly hope to see accomplished. We shall, therefore, cordially rejoice if the gentleman to whom we refer, and who in experience, taste and judgment is second to none, can succeed in so wedding "High Art" to the Art that has been in this country considered and treated as "Low Art" so as to commence a new era for both.' Henry Cole's patronage and ideas were a vital influence in the years when machines and mass production threatened to stifle good taste with the sheer dead weight of industry. His Christmas card was to be an acorn from which much grew. He served on the executive committee for the Great Exhibition of 1851, and became the first Director of what is now the Victoria and Albert Museum.

In 1848 another Christmas card was designed by William Egley, a painter celebrated for his portrayal of the crowded interior of a London omnibus. Both Horsley's and Egley's cards were for private use only and it was not until 1862 that Messrs Goodall & Sons made the first issue of Christmas cards to the trade. The designs were of holly, mistletoe and robins. John Leighton was the designer and his choice of the robin as the Christmas bird may well have been influenced by the nickname of 'robins' given to the red-jacketed postmen who would deliver the cards. Goodall & Sons, however, were not to become the giants of the Christmas card trade and within a few years they had sold this side of their business to Marcus Ward & Company who were to take the Christmas card vogue to great heights.

In many aspects the early Christmas cards were very similar to the earlier valentines with their lace paper, doors that revealed interior festivities, and double cards opening out to form nativity scenes. Many designs for Christmas and New Year cards, as well as for calendars, came from the hand of Kate Greenaway. The majority of her cards were published by Messrs Ward & Company until they ended their business relationship in 1878. Kate Greenaway's work was particularly favoured by the public at large, although it was seldom related to the festive season. Her cards with innocent, happy children in their distinctive clothing are in constant demand by collectors.

During the 1880s De La Rue published a series of Christmas cards by W.S. Coleman depicting nude or scantily dressed maidens, and these too are collected today. Yet, as is invariably the case,

ABOVE Christmas card sachet by E. Rimmel with the exterior of a theatre opening to reveal a pantomime in progress, *c.* 1870

LEFT Two mid-Victorian Christmas cards

it is the cards that most readily reflect their period that are regarded as the most satisfying prizes. With some quarter million different cards produced during the Victorian era the field for the collector is rich and fertile, to say the least, and there is much scope for speculation.

Christmas cards were also produced by Thomas Stevens; colour printed on thin card and edged with silk they were sold as 'Stevens New Silk Edged Perfumed Cards'.

Playing cards

The origin of playing cards is uncertain. They may have originated in the East as many authorities have stated although the Eastern games were very different from those of the West. The first reference to cards occurs in the writings of a German monk who, in 1377, comments briefly, '. . . a certain game called the game of cards has come to us in this year'. References to cards occur shortly afterwards in manuscripts all over Europe. If, as some have stated, the game was brought back by returning crusaders, then we would certainly have heard of them at an earlier date. The first cards used in Europe were hand painted, and therefore card games became the pastime of the rich. The public at large was unable to obtain them until cards were printed on large sheets by the woodblock method, coloured and then cut up into packs. The packs have always been divided into four suits but these were of far greater variety and very different from the suits today. Just as the first printed books concentrated upon religion, heraldry and falconry, so too in a way did playing cards. One of the oldest hand-painted packs in Europe is displayed in Vienna and the suits are divided into Hounds, Herons, Falcons and Lures.

The establishment of suits was an involved process. Some people believe that they represented the main divisions of the population, that is, the Church, the aristocracy (which automatically included military power), the merchant class and the peasantry. In turn, these classes were symbolized, in Italy at least, by chalices, swords, money and clubs. Anne of Cleves did much to promote the use of cards at the English court.

Playing cards used in Britain were based on the French packs, and the court cards used today are still to some extent derived from the old court dress of France. Britain also used the same symbols as the French to represent each suit. A pack printed in Rouen during the 16th century provided the basis for packs used today in the English-speaking world. Eastern cards, some of them circular, are very different from the European and are not often found.

A duty was imposed on all imported playing cards after Charles I granted a charter to the Worshipful Company of Makers of Playing Cards in 1628.

One of the aids to dating old playing cards is the identification of the method used to print them. The first hand-painted cards are exceptionally rare and often very exceptional works of art in their own right. Woodblock engraving was used during the 18th century and well into the 19th century but by then some manufacturers were using the technique of chromolithography and today many cards are produced on the latest web-offset printing machines. Handling and comparing cards printed by different methods will quickly bring confidence in determining the method used for a particular card. One of the first things to strike the new collector is that, until the later years of the 19th century, playing cards were square shouldered; the rounded corners which we now take for granted in a modern pack were a late innovation. The reason for the square corners is that, as mentioned earlier, they were cut out of large sheets by hand. For the same reason the margins around the old hand-cut cards vary in size. The cards themselves also tend to be handsomely wider than cards today. Colouring was applied to the blocked designs either by hand or by the use of a stencil, although many early cards were uncoloured. It will also be noticed that until the middle of the 19th century most court cards from British packs are standing, full-length figures. Some double-headed cards were produced in the early part of the century but it was after 1850 that the double-headed card became accepted as standard.

Playing cards have long been used for fortune-telling and it is the Tarot packs that are most often associated with this. Tarot was very much a game until its application for other purposes, and these cards, their use and history, are a separate interest for those who wish to pursue it.

One of the particularly interesting areas of card collecting that has attracted many people to the subject, are the packs printed for political, satirical, commemorative, or other ends. A Presidential pack was issued for J.F. Kennedy and Presidents Nixon, Carter and Reagan all appear on playing cards. At least one 'Victory' pack marked the end of the war in Europe in 1945 and there may well have been others. All manner of historical personages have made their appearance on court cards. Immediately following the French Revolution the kings and queens fled the French packs to be replaced by Liberty and Fraternity, but it was not long before the aristocrats were once again returned to the playing cards. Cards have been used as money and as teaching aids; in fact, they have for many centuries been closely linked with the affairs of man. If it had not been for the attachment of Lord Sandwich to the gambling table and his playing cards, so much so that he refused to leave them for meals, no one would have brought him a slice of beef between two slices of bread and we would not have had the sandwich!

Since the recent discovery of considerable quantities of mid-19th century playing cards in the stock drawers of an old business on the Continent, it should now be possible to obtain specimen cards of this period very reasonably.

RIGHT Mid 19th-century playing cards showing the characteristic square corners and block printed designs

Books and photographs

Victorian bookbindings

With the growing enthusiasm for Victoriana it was perhaps obvious that the quality and interest of publishers' bookbindings of the last century would soon be recognized. Interest in the subject rapidly developed during the 1970s and this has had the effect of raising values, but many good bindings may still be obtained reasonably and representative collections formed.

The work of the individual bookbinder is an entirely separate field from that being considered here, and far more costly. When printed books first made their appearance in the mid-15th century it was the practice for the purchaser to have his book bound in the manner he desired. Identifying the work of these early bookbinders and binderies frequently calls for considerable scholarship as well as a deep purse, which may be another good reason for turning to the 19th century to exercise one's bibliomania.

Many of the 19th-century bookbinders pasted a small label, or printed their name directly, on work they were responsible for. Although craft bindings do not readily fall into the category we are discussing here, there is one that collectors would do well to watch for.

The words 'Bound by F. Bedford' usually found stamped on an endpaper denote a craftsman of remarkable quality who specialized in binding slim volumes in carefully chosen full calf with gilt decorated spines. One of Bedford's great book collecting patrons was Fredrick Locker Lampson who created the famous Rowfant Library. Locker Lampson used fondly to describe his binder as 'the emperor of morocco'.

A great revolution in book design occurred when the publisher William Pickering first began to use cloth for bookbinding during the 1820s, probably on an 1825 edition of the works of Dr. Johnson. Individual embroidered bindings had been used centuries before, but the cloth used by Pickering was little more than calico dress material with paper labels pasted on. Seven years later John Murray was publishing books with their titles in gold lettering stamped directly on to the cloth. Murray published an edition of the works of Lord Byron in 1832, the first two volumes having their titles on paper labels pasted on while the third was printed on to the cloth. This method was invented by Alexander Leighton, one of the commercial bookbinders. A factory was started in Hoxton for the production of cloth specially prepared for bookbinding, and by 1840 cloth for permanent bookbinding was becoming as firmly established as the traditional calf.

A single movement by a machine stamping designs from a brass plate on to the cloth could now achieve the visual effect of the painstaking hand tooling carried out in the leather bindings. It brought in a whole new era in book design and production. Wages were low, industrial strength was growing, and imported raw materials often cost little. These were all circumstances that combined to make possible books of sumptuous and exciting bindings that such ordinary trade editions

A collection of cloth, wood, and calf bindings that demonstrate well Victorian taste in commercial bookbinding during the second half of the 19th century

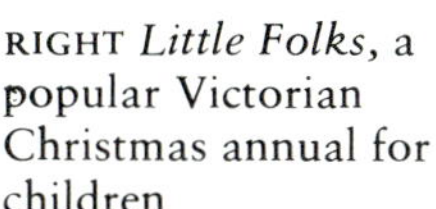

RIGHT *Little Folks,* a popular Victorian Christmas annual for children

FAR RIGHT *Wordsworth Poems,* a beautiful example of a publisher's binding using deep purple crushed morocco inset with a silk-woven panel by Thomas Stevens, surrounded by a tortoise-shell border

will never be seen again. With colour printing being used in typography as well as illustration, the mid-19th century saw the production of what must surely be some of the most beautiful books ever printed in the world.

For the Victorian middle class it was the new, well-bound gift book that proved the great attraction and these now provide a rich area for collectors; the bindings of such books tend to be far better suited to the display cabinet rather than the bookshelf. In the second half of the 19th century increasing numbers of designers began to sign their bindings, although many good bindings are seen that bear no signature at all. When signatures do appear they are often in the form of initials, and bindings need to be closely scrutinized in order to find them; frequently they are half hidden in the design itself.

The initials most frequently noted are those of John Leighton, which may even appear several times on one binding. Leighton, although credited with putting the first robin on a Christmas card in 1862, was perhaps not a great designer but was extremely competent, interesting and highly industrious. As one of the earliest commercial artists he turned his hand to almost any graphic work that came his way, from books to bank notes. If not very original, Leighton was certainly versatile. He explored the use of countersunk designs which were stamped onto the binding and created a binding on two levels.

There was also a fashion at this time for setting pictorial paper panels in the middle of cloth bindings and such examples must have an important place in any collection. Such panels vary in shape but ovals and almond shapes are those most frequently met with. Signed panels are rare and should be looked for.

The styles and materials used in Victorian bookbinding are legion: carved wood very frequently in a Gothic style, papier mâché, terracotta, vulcanite, bronzed metal, mother-of-pearl, tortoise-shell, morocco, cloth, embossed leather, silk, hardstones, even timber from sunken ships or from the doors of some notorious prison. Many continental bindings are also well worthy of consideration.

The later bindings of the 19th century by such artists as Ricketts, Housman, and Aubrey Beardsley, began to break new ground yet again and in so doing heralded a new century. Such books reflect their period, occasionally look beyond it, and possess a wealth of fascinating detail enough to satisfy the collecting appetites of the most demanding connoisseur. Victorian bindings hold their surprises and trace the social, artistic, and industrial developments of their time.

Contrasting 19th-century bindings including Volume 1 of *The Yellow Book,* designed by Aubrey Beardsley, which was to have such far reaching effects on graphic design

Victorian illustrated books

When the very English art form of watercolour drawing was achieving its golden age of accomplishment and success at the end of the 18th

The Parables of Our Lord, a superb example of chromolithography by Henry Noel Humphreys, 1846

century, the skills of aquatint engraving also came into their own. Aquatint engravings have the appearance of wash drawings, and they give surface 'tone' to an etching. They did much to stimulate interest in the further development of colour printing in 19th-century book production. Many technical innovations, however, were in hand. Aloys Senefelder (1771–1834) took out the first patent for lithography in Britain in 1800. He had made a series of experiments in Bavaria that led to the discovery that if prepared limestone was polished it could be drawn on with greasy lithographic ink or crayons (see page 31). However, it was during the first decade of Queen Victoria's reign that lithographs were established in book illustration. The first book with lithographic illustrations is dated 1807 in J.T. Smith's *Antiquities of Westminster.* While Victorian book illustration is of great variety and range, comment here is directed in the main towards colour printing, often very beautiful and most likely to catch the eye of the majority of collectors.

Lithographs in full colour became known as chromolithographs and were eventually to be produced from metal plates rather than from the stone. Chromolithograph was the name used by G. Engelmann to describe the technique patented by him in 1837. Initially the individual colours were applied to the paper by using a series of lithographic stones or zinc plates in succession, but later a machine was developed making low-priced mass production possible. Because of the wide interest now being shown in Victorian colour printing the early examples of fine chromolithography are becoming somewhat rare and costly.

Unlike most antiques or works of art that have an instant visual impact upon the person looking at them, most books require opening for the appreciation of text and illustration. It is for this reason that fine books will continue to appear on second-hand bookstalls, and appreciation and diligence may well be rewarded by an important discovery.

The most magnificent of the colour-printed books are decorated throughout very much in the manner of medieval manuscripts; it is this type of book that is properly referred to as being 'illuminated'. Many other Victorian volumes only have coloured ornaments or illuminated title pages. Collectors seeking a deeper knowledge of 19th-century book production will find *Victorian Book Design and Colour Printing*, by Ruari McLean, published by Faber and Faber, 1963, 1972, an indispensable volume.

There are certain Victorian designers and illustrators whose work should be kept well in mind. The Welsh architect, Owen Jones (1809–74), established an important lithographic press in London, and perhaps his most celebrated work is monumental *The Grammar of Ornament* published in 1856.

Henry Noel Humphreys (1810–79) had a major influence on Victorian illuminated books. He had studied in Italy and had become fascinated by Italian art and the study of early illuminated manuscripts. His *Parables of Our Lord* published in 1847 and *The Miracles of Our Lord* published the following year are very desirable books indeed. Although inspired by the products of the medieval monastic scriptoriums, Humphreys was no copyist and the versatility of his illustrations and decorations have a surprising freshness, which he clearly sought to achieve. At the end of *Parables* he states: 'In illuminating the sacred Parables contained in this volume, it has been the aim of the designer to render the ornamental borderings of each page appropriate to the text, and to avoid all mere arbitrary or idle ornaments; and he has thought it more suitable that the garments of gold and many colours in which he has arrayed them should at all events be *new* rather than embroidery borrowed from old missals or other sources of conventional ornament, however quaint or beautiful; and therefore, however far the illuminator may have fallen short of his intention, the designs will be found to be strictly original, fresh, and full of the purpose alone to which they are devoted.'

When Messrs Longman published Humphreys' *Sentiments and Similes of William Shakespeare* during the year of the Great Exhibition, he stated his case in the preface in a manner that shows his awareness of literature and of the technological advances open to him in printing and book design and production.

'When I first thought of producing an example of book decorations, as the result of my studies in the "Art of Illumination", I at once selected the present subject, as the vehicle to receive my projected embellishments; for to what purpose could the latest refinements in decorative printing be more appropriately devoted than the embellishment of a series of selections from the writings of our immortal Shakespeare? With this feeling I have gathered together some of the gems of thought of our great poet, and endeavoured to range them worthily in a fitting casket – to enshrine them, as it were, in a reliquary as rich as a combination of the typographic and lithochromic arts could form. . . . Progress in various kinds of printing has enabled the press to rival the art of the illuminator himself, and the highly enriched bordering round the first page of this book is entirely the result of this new application of art.'

The Poems of Oliver Goldsmith, illustrated by Birket Foster and Henry Noel Humphreys, and printed by Edmund Evans, 1860

George Baxter (1804–67) is celebrated for his invention of a method of printing in oil inks. He used a key-plate engraving in a neutral colour followed by metal or wood blocks to carry each colour impression. Baxter would have used from ten to twenty printings to create each print and on a few occasions he may have used more. Most of his work was published on stamped mounts which usually carry his address and are thus useful in dating them. Only a handful of books have Baxter illustrations. The earliest are simple vignettes for the title pages of Mudie's two volumes *Feathered Tribes of the British Islands* 1834, and the frontispiece to Mudie's *The Natural History of Birds*, also published in 1834.

Many of Baxter's plates and blocks were sold to licensees but some of them surpassed his colour effects. Subjected to strong light Baxter prints tend to fade alarmingly.

From 1850 colour printing from wood blocks became a major activity. George Leighton (1826–95), a cousin of John Leighton who created so many of the designs for bindings, was a colour printer of considerable talent. He had been apprenticed to George Baxter and his illustrations to Palgrave's *Gems of English Art* contain twenty-four prints of great quality.

J. M. Kronheim (1810–96), was one of the licensees of the Baxter process and he also worked in chronolithography. He did the illustrations in oil colours for an 1861 edition of *Robinson Crusoe* which is one of the first editions of this story, first published in 1719, to have colour. Another attractive example of Kronheim printing is *Thompson's Poetical Works* of 1869.

Books illustrated by Edmund Evans (1826–1905) are particularly sought after, and with good reason. He had a lifelong friendship with Birket Foster (1825–99) an artist who delighted in portraying the English countryside and whose work exudes nostalgia. Because of Birket Foster's technique and eye for close detail he was often referred to as 'the guinea-an-inch painter'. Evans interpreted such work with great sympathy and, in *The Poems of Oliver Goldsmith* published in 1859, Foster's watercolours and the engraving art of Evans came together magnificently.

The period to which all these people belong was also the last years of hand-work in mass commercial illustration; the challenge of photography had finally won through.

It should be remembered that the illustrators of children's books have long attracted collectors. Kate Greenaway and Beatrix Potter are typical but not inexpensive examples; in recent years the work of Ernest Shepard, illustrator of *Winnie-the-Pooh*, has been commanding increasing attention. So too have the book illustrations of Edward Ardizzone who died in 1980.

School prize books

School prize books form an important field that has been sadly overlooked by book collectors. In many book shops two identical 19th-century editions of, say, *Robinson Crusoe* may well be priced differently, the copy in plain calf with a price of £10, the other again in calf but bearing the arms of a college or grammar school, will very likely be several pounds less. As the decades roll by, however, areas of collecting are re-assessed and prize books are now regarded with far more favour than they were previously. The reasons for this are not hard to find. In today's terms they are expensively bound; in fact, the cost of such prizes would be prohibitive for most schools today. Living as we do in the final quarter of the 20th century we are passing through a period of much change in our educational system. Indeed, many of the schools and colleges that once issued such volumes are no more, and such rewards for conduct, or academic achievement have come to be regarded by many as elitist and outmoded.

Between the late 15th century and 1660, hundreds of grammar schools were established in England. The realization of the necessity to support education was becoming widespread, and private individuals were readily making their wealth available at a time when schools of some importance might be both built and endowed for between £500 and £1000. The schools sought to bring learning to boys of all backgrounds and their catchment area embraced the entire kingdom. A directive to a school in 1519 stipulated the duty to teach '. . . all such scolers of men children . . . as shall resorte for lernyng and noon other indifferently after their capacities as well as the poore mannes child as the riche.' Six years later Manchester Grammar School was proclaiming that '. . . no scollar nor infaunt, of what cuntrey or schire so ever he be of, beyng man child, be refused. . . .'

The brief reign of Edward VI, an educated and precocious child, did much to stimulate the growth of education and many schools were founded in his name. The charter of Edward VI Free Grammar School at Louth, Lincolnshire, granted in 1551, expresses well the exciting urgency that was being felt for the pursuit of learning: 'Whereas We have always coveted, with a most exceeding, vehement, and ardent desire, that good Literature and Discipline might be diffused and propagated, through all the parts of our Kingdom, as wherein the best government and administration of affairs consists; and therefore, with no small ernest have We been intent on the liberal institution of Youth, that it might be brought up to Science, in places of our Kingdom most proper and suitable for such functions; it being, as it were, the Foundation and growth of our Commonwealth, and having certain and unquestionable knowledge that our Town of Louth, in our County of Lincoln, is a place most proper and fit for the teaching and instructing of children and youth, in regard it is very populous and stocked with youth, and, heretofore, a great concourse of children and youth have flocked thither, from adjacent Towns, to acquire learning.'

The building-up of even a modest collection of prize volumes very soon begins to reflect and reveal this sweeping panorama of educational history; not only do the arms and the seals of the schools, stamped in gold on natural or tinted calf, and the titles of the books chosen, reflect period and taste, but also the signatures of form masters and headmasters reveal the names of some of the great educationists of the past. Occasionally the name of the schoolboy recipient will reveal a man who was to make his mark in the arts or sciences.

The life and correspondence of Dr Thomas Arnold of Rugby School was a popular prize chosen by headmasters for senior boys. The classics were an obvious choice and so too were many aspects of history – Macaulay's *History of England* and Layard's *Discovery of Nineveh* for example. Histories of ancient cities such as Winchester were frequently given, and so were works of natural history, of which the most popular of all was Gilbert White's *The Natural History of Selborne*, a regular prize for the students of Cheltenham College.

Fine prize books were by no means the prerogative of private education. The Liverpool Institute Commercial School in 1880 issued well chosen works in bindings emblazoned with the emblems of the Institute. Many prize bindings bear the famous arms of Merchant Companies such as George Watson's Ladies College in Edinburgh and the arms of the cathedral schools today form most desirable acquisitions. Hereford College School, for example, gave important books

A collection of Victorian Prize books, including prizes awarded by The Royal Hospital School, Greenwich; Cheltenham College; Uppingham Grammar School; King Edwards School, Louth and Hereford College School

in the field of science as well as theology, and Kings School, Ely favoured volumes on history and manufacturing skills.

The 19th century was a period of great discovery and many volumes containing early photographs were chosen as prize books. Before 1875 some 500 titles were illustrated with real photographs applied to the page by hand. One such book, *Leslie's Hand Book For Young Painters* by the Royal Academician C. R. Leslie, author of *The Life of Constable*, was given as a drawing prize at the City of London School in 1859; the book itself was printed in 1855 and contains one of the earliest photographs of a painting by Rembrandt. The photographer was the now-celebrated Joseph Cundall of 168, New Bond Street in London. To find photography used as illustration in a book dealing with painting at that time is rare indeed.

Twenty years later photographic illustration was far more widespread although photographs were still applied by hand. A good example is the 1877 edition of Longfellow's works, which also was favoured as a prize book. A valued copy in the author's collection was presented by the Commissioners of Intermediate Education for Ireland in 1879.

The inscriptions to be found in these books throw much light on the sentiments and morals as well as the history of the day.

A star atlas, a prize given at Wesleyan College, Taunton, was presented 'For Distingished Answering on Mr Todd's Protestant Lectures'.

Twenty years on, the Vicar of Weston presented a copy of *Sir John Franklin and the Romance of the North West Passage* to Master Frank Glover, with the charming lines:

from one who's a lover
of Franklyn the Rover.
If Frankie would prove a
good man, and discover
the secret of fame,
and a well honoured name,
he must sail through this volume
from cover to cover.

EHH

Weston Vicarage
Xmas 1895

Reading the labels in prize books one is aware that all prize-givings were special occasions and, occasionally, a book will come to hand that shows that they could also be extra special. For example, prize books were clearly commemorative objects and a copy of 'William Watson's Collected Poems' of 1899 was used as a prize at the North London Collegiate School for Girls the following year. The distribution of prizes on the 25 June 1900 marked the Jubilee Year of the school and the books were presented to the pupils by H.R.H. the Princess of Wales.

There is an extraordinary sense of pleasure to be experienced when handling a beautifully bound book and so many prize books fall into that category. They illuminate the struggles and the ideals of education, and if the collector selects his titles and bindings carefully he will be rewarded with a collection of some of the great books of the past, many of which contain truths and discoveries as relevant to us now as when first printed. Prize books have a long tradition and it is still possible to find, in second-hand and antiquarian book shops, vellum-bound works bearing the arms of continental universities and awarded in the 17th century.

How pleasant it is to take down from a bookseller's shelf a volume of Southey, as the author did recently, and to find that its first recipient was a young man at King's College in 1837 and that the book had been awarded to him by the then Archbishop of Canterbury. It is at such moments that a sense of continuity and appreciation is at its greatest.

Old photographs

W. H. Fox Talbot (1800–1877) of Lacock Abbey in Wiltshire achieved the first successful photographic process on paper in 1834. The small negative, the oldest in existence, of his photograph of an oriel window in the abbey, is now preserved in the Science Museum. It was pioneer work that provided the stimulus for one of the most useful inventions of all time.

Living as we do in a century of great social upheaval and scientific and technological development, the years before 1914 appear from old photographs to have been a different world. There is no town or village that has not incurred change and, suddenly, the old photograph has become as much of a historical document as an early manuscript, and is sometimes a work of art into the bargain. Before the 19th century had run its course, people were able to look back through their photographs and see themselves a whole generation away, their image caught in time. The early photographers experienced many technical difficulties, particularly in the 'fixing' of a photograph, and so many Victorian photographs are like old soldiers in that they simply fade away. As the century advanced various processes were introduced to stop this happening, the best known of them being the 'Woodburytype'.

Certain of the early photographers have become much celebrated today. In 1974 an album containing the work of Mrs Julia Margaret Cameron (1815–79), perhaps the most famous amateur portrait photographer ever, was sold in London for £52,000. That album, containing her portraits of so many of the great personalities of her day, is now safely housed in the National Portrait Gallery. Mrs Cameron had sent the album as a gift to Sir John Herschel astronomer, scientist and inventor, who discovered hypo and coined the terms 'negative' and 'positive'.

Old photographs are packed with interest. It is seldom that a 'bad' photograph is seen, the reason being that taking a photograph in the 19th century was always an occasion rather than the instant commonplace occurrence the photograph has become today. You only have to look at individual portraits or group photographs to see that most subjects look well pleased with themselves, waistcoats and watchchains thrust well forward, and very much aware that the photograph was an important event in their lives.

Unfortunately, far too many photographers tended to photograph the same things, just as they do today. Thousands of old photographs will be found of cathedrals, main streets and civic dignitaries. Very few photographs set out to capture the way ordinary folk lived, life below stairs, craftsmen using the tools of their trade, children at play, fishermen and farms. These form a major area for photograph collectors. Another important field is among the town and village scenes that demonstrate dramatic change in housing development, transport and costume. The publishing of photographic histories of towns and villages has now become something of an industry, and fascinating and important sources they are too.

Historic events are clearly of major importance. Original photographs taken during the Crimean War and the American Civil War are obviously important to our knowledge and of considerable monetary value. The Boer War and the Spanish Civil War all yielded outstanding photographs. Photographs exist of Winston Churchill as a prisoner of the Boers. An original photograph would be particularly valuable because of the manner in which the remarkable career of Churchill developed, and the interest of a large body of collectors who seek out all objects associated with the great man.

Many homes in Britain must contain family albums containing pictures depicting life in India in the days of the British Raj. Such albums reflect history in a way that few other things are able to do. Albums such as these are just as likely to turn up in the local jumble sales as they are in a London auction room, and collectors will do well to keep a sharp eye open. In spite of the considerable publicity that has been given to old photographs, thousands of photographs tucked away in old drawers and albums must be destroyed each year through lack of awareness or sheer ignorance. How often do we still hear of the bonfires where 'it took days to burn all the old letters and photographs the old folk had hoarded for years'?

The period of World War II, now that we have

Two cabinet size and six carte-de-visite Victorian photographs, including a little known portrait of Charles Darwin

A set of twelve mounted photographs showing the phases of the moon, by Smith, Beck & Beck from an original negative by Warren De La Rue, 1861–70. Until man's venture into space these were among the best photographs available of the moon

An ivory inlaid Victorian photograph album

moved a generation in time away from it, is attracting intense interest. Although it was not always easy to obtain film and there were many areas where photography was prohibited, amateur photographers obtained many important pictures. A christening photograph taken in a garden with a child and proud parents in the foreground, and an air-raid shelter in the background, is of historic and human interest. A wedding group photographed on the pavement may also show a blast-wall and a poster exhorting its readers to 'Dig for Victory'; of such stuff history is made.

The Victorians were great photograph collectors and few homes would have been without an album on the sideboard. Many were cheap but others were costly symbols of wealth made of many materials from silver and velvet to lacquer and tortoise-shell. They were designed with great ingenuity and in rich variety and most of them were fitted with heavy clasps and locks. Such albums are well worth collecting in their own right. Many postcard albums were also produced in similar grand style.

It was not only family photographs that were kept in albums. During the 1860s a collecting craze developed for small portrait photographs known as cartes-de-visite. The original pictures measure about 8.5 x 6 cm ($3\frac{1}{2}$ x $2\frac{1}{2}$ in) and were mounted on cards that were slightly larger, although smaller sizes are seen from time to time. Queen Victoria and Prince Albert were highly popular, so too was Gladstone. A Victorian galaxy of writers, poets, statesmen, aristocrats and actors were all on the cartes-de-visite. Some of the portraits are commonly found and Charles Dickens is a good example; portraits of Charles Darwin, on the other hand, are rare. The Victorians did not neglect the carte-de-visite portraits of their family and friends and neither should the collector of today. Unless the old photographs actually have the name of the sitter inscribed on them, it is unlikely that the individuals will ever be identified. However, portraits of unknowns may still reveal fashion detail or studio furnishings, and those of men in uniform are particularly interesting. Collecting the work of the early photographers of one's home town or county can be rewarding, and the backs of the cartes-de-visite are usually beautifully printed with decorations or statements to the effect that the picture had been obtained by 'Instantaneous Photograph'. Other photographs proudly proclaim that they are also 'Photographers to H.R.H. The Prince of Wales', etc.

Photographic equipment manufactured prior to 1930 has also become part of the growing enthusiasm for collecting in this field. The literature on the subject should not be neglected, the Centenary Exhibition catalogue '100 Years of Photography 1839–1939' held at The Science Museum, South Kensington in the summer of 1939 is of great interest. A study of the lives of the photographic pioneers and of the processes they introduced is essential to any serious collecting. The men whose work should be particularly studied are Joseph Niépce (1765–1833), Louis Daguerre (1789–1854), Henry Fox Talbot (1800–1877), and Sir John Herschel (1792–1871).

The name of Mrs Julia M. Cameron has already been mentioned but other photographers whose work should be examined are David Octavius Hill, Roger Fenton, Henry Peach Robinson and Oscar Rejlander. Rejlander made one of the first attempts to produce a large and elaborate photograph. The result, in 1857, was an extraordinary print made from thirty different negatives. He called it 'Two Ways of Life', representing the pagan as nude and the Christian as fully clothed!

Good original photographs of all periods are worth a place in a collection and, when searching through antique markets, stalls and junk shops, it is always possible that old Victorian glass negatives or photographic slides for projection by magic lantern might be picked up reasonably. Very often fine prints may be obtained from these. Many old postcards are simply a small issue of original photographs and these, probably the work of some local photographer recording, say, the destruction of a pier or widespread flooding in a town or an early political meeting, can be important items.

A word of warning. Just as copies and fakes have bedevilled most fields in which collectors are interested, it should be remembered that photography is no exception. As values of good photographs increase so will the temptation to the unscrupulous to employ original methods to produce authentic looking prints.

Jewellery

All civilizations have made and worn jewellery. Like costume, such personal adornments denoted position, wealth and power. Early jewellery may be worth a fortune and fine pieces of all later periods are costly, but here we are concerned with the 19th century, and examples that are both attractive and historically interesting, yet all too frequently overlooked.

As the Industrial Revolution moved into a higher gear so the Victorian middle class developed in prosperity. The Reform Bill of 1832 had already charted the way to political power. It was an age of overpowering respectability and pretentious display, as well as a time of commercial and industrial expansion. A 'sense of possession' was highly developed among Victorian families and it was the ideal environment for the production of jewellery to flourish. Birmingham became the renowned manufacturing centre for cheap jewellery and it supplied Britain, the Empire, and many foreign markets too. Mass production methods also improved the supply of fine jewellery. For the man of expanding property, seeking status in his community and business, a wife well-jewelled made the point emphatically. The wide and adventurous range of jewellery that developed in the 19th century was linked, as always, to the mode of costume then fashionable, so tastes in jewellery changed as rapidly as dress. Many prospective purchasers of Victorian jewellery tend to judge its appeal to them by the prevailing tastes and times in which they live, but the collector would do well to consider such pieces in the light of the fashions for which they were first developed; this will also assist the accurate dating of jewellery.

Memorial jewellery

This class of jewellery became widely popular during the second half of the 18th century and through much of the Victorian era, although the fashion for such things had originated much earlier. Following the Restoration a quantity of jewellery rapidly made its appearance in memory of Charles I. Small portraits woven in human hair set in enamel surrounds depicted the late monarch. Today, of course, these are valuable rarities and unlikely to be encountered outside major collections and museums. Memorial pendants were also made of enamel in the form of a miniature human skull.

In the 20th century western society has failed somewhat in its readiness to look at death and mourning with such directness as previous generations have done. Many people consider memorial jewellery as being 'not very nice', particularly where hair is used as ornament. This attitude of dismissing memorial jewellery in such summary fashion usually indicates that the historical and social background it represents has been neither explored nor understood. A careful examination of such pieces will invariably reveal fine craftsmanship, although the later Victorian mass-produced pieces always look precisely what they are. Mourning rings form a substantial part of memorial jewellery. On the death of Samuel Pepys, the goldsmith Richard Moore was instructed by the Pepys family's banker to make mourning rings for distribution to family and friends. Very soon it had become commonplace for a man to set aside money so that rings might be worn in his memory; it was all a rather attractive expression of sentimental regard, and these rings today are not uncommon. The neo-classical churchyard sculptures and church memorials depicting scenes such as a widow mourning at the side of a tomb usually surmounted by an urn, was also a scene much painted on small ivory and enamel panels for use as clasps and pendants, most of them oval in shape.

Memorial jewellery made for the famous is very much sought after. Most mourning rings carry

Whitby jet became highly fashionable with the Victorians as mourning jewellery (as did hair jewellery). Small fossil ammonites were frequently mounted in brooches and are often referred to as fossil jewellery. The central brooch with its bezel of hair surrounded by seed pearls and coral is a style that became popular in the late 18th century

inscriptions on the inside face and this gives an undoubted sense of individuality and character to each ring; pendants, books and bracelet clasps tend to be inscribed in the same manner. John Miers (1758–1812) probably the finest profilist of the 18th century, advertised in 1783 that he carried out profile likenesses 'upon ivory for rings'. To achieve such a silhouette with accuracy he would have first taken a larger profile and reduced it with the aid of a pantograph, much as a draftsman might reduce the scale of a drawing today. Gold, black enamel and seed pearls became most associated with such jewellery during the 19th century, and the use of plaited human hair in the bezel of rings and in pendants also became widespread in the production of hair necklaces and hair bracelets. Some of the very finest hair work of this kind was made between 1840 and 1860. Landscape pictures were even made in hair, and in the Paris Exposition of 1855 a life-size hair portrait of Queen Victoria became a focal point for visitors.

Most of the hair jewellery produced was the work of professionals, but it was also an art adopted by many young ladies themselves for it was felt that the hair of a loved relative or friend might all too easily be substituted for another. In fact it should not be thought that all hair jewellery is of a memorial nature. A magazine of the 1850s called *The Family Friend* gave its readers do-it-yourself instructions in making all manner of things with hair. Watchguards, hair nets, hair rings were all enthusiastically encouraged. For the making of a hair bracelet it was necessary to 'Prepare thirty-two strands of twenty-four hairs each . . . and arrange them on a table in eight groups of four.' The instructions also observed that 'twenty or thirty inch hair' would be required for the completion of such a bracelet. They also recommended that 'A serpent's or bird's head with jewelled eyes, forms a pretty finish; but this is of course a matter of taste.'

Occasionally, a woman would make a watch-chain from her hair as a special gift to her husband-to-be, so it was also clear that hair used was by no means only taken from the deceased. Hair jewellery was so much in demand during the middle years of the century that 'artists in hair', as they were known, had all manner of devices from a simple curl to 'Prince of Wales Feathers' already made up in various colours to supply a customer's requirements instantly. The handling of hair jewellery is very pleasant indeed, much of it retaining a surprising elasticity. Anyone wishing to make hair jewellery of their own would do well to seek out a rare volume with the title *The Lock of Hair*, by Alexanna Speight, 1872. Hair jewellery was never popular outside England.

Jet

Jet is a variety of lignite or coal and when lit it will burn. Artefacts of many kinds were made from jet by the people of prehistory, but it had the longest popularity in Spain where it was used for amulets and devotional objects from the 10th to the 19th centuries. Spanish jet, however, was softer than that found in Britain; it tended to split and flake and it did not last long. In Britain it was the jet found at Whitby that achieved the height of fashion soon after it began being carved in the early 19th century. This black coal, hard enough to cut, facet and polish became known as Whitby jet and it is still often referred to as such today.

John Carter and Robert Jefferson began a jet-carving and turning industry in the early 19th century, which very soon began to flourish. Black being the colour for mourning, the demand for jet brooches, necklaces and crucifixes was constant. With the death of Prince Albert jet reached its pinnacle of popularity. Soon after it began to decline somewhat in public favour and it never recovered. Today there is little demand for jet, but such a situation is not the time for rejecting but for collecting.

Whitby jet was once exported all over the world, and there can be no doubt that the day will come when fine examples of jet craftsmanship will again be sought after. Jet is light in weight and the best pieces are a lustrous black. Sometimes the growth rings of the tree, part of which it once was, can be identified. Black glass sold as jet together with a decline in workmanship and above all in design probably speeded its fall from favour. Some jet necklaces were carved from the solid in one piece!

Ivory, claws and fossils

The 'Victorians' love of jewellery and ornament led to the exploration of many avenues. That they should have chosen ivory is perhaps not unexpected. Many mammals produce this beautiful white material but in the 19th century the exploration of Africa was proceeding apace and tusk-carrying elephants were falling in their thousands to the elephant hunters' guns. Ivory was the counterpart of jet. Splendid ivory pieces were being carved between 1850 and 1870; animal brooches often carved with deer, plain and carved ivory rings, and beautiful ear-rings carved with ivy leaves and other naturalistic subjects.

Animal and bird claws, and animal paws were all mounted as brooches during the second half of the 19th century but clearly they are not to the taste of everyone. Outstanding among such pieces are the complete sets consisting of tigers' claws mounted in gold, and forming necklace, bracelet pendant and ear-rings. Such items lose their lustre with the realization of the ruthless hunting that was carried out to supply the raw materials. Grouse-foot and other bird claw brooches were also very popular.

Fossil hunting was a more gentle pursuit and fine, well-matched fossils were frequently mounted in either gold or silver, ammonites being the principal fossils used for this purpose.

Cameos, lava and mosaics

Italy was beloved by the Victorian traveller and it is not surprising that the jewellery of the Mediterranean should have made such a firm impact on popular Victorian taste. Fine cameos are still being carved today and unless seen in their original mounts they can be extremely difficult to date. The best cameos were often set in somewhat intricate gold mounts of filigree, but as the century progressed so machine-pressed thin gold mounts with leaf and scroll designs captured the bulk of the market. Gem cameos were and are, of course, highly prized as jewels and therefore costly. Here we deal with the shell cameo which, though reasonably easy to obtain, may vary greatly in quality. The centre for shell-cameo carving has always been Naples. The shells used today are the horned helmet, King helmet, Red helmet and Queen Conch, found from the Caribbean to the Indian Ocean; various cowrie and mussel shells have also been used.

The large helmet shells are the most important and it was from these that the majority of Victorian cameos were carved. Some helmet shells have been carved with pictorial subjects so that the entire shell or pair of shells may be used as table or cabinet ornaments, rather than being cut and mounted for personal adornment. The finest cameos are always carved from the finest shells, that is, with coloured layers right through so that good contrasting colours may be obtained. The shells are a very hard form of mother-of-pearl and often require special tools for carving. The designs are mainly classical in derivation and therefore somewhat repetitive but in popularity they have well and truly stood the test of time. The collector should look for the well-carved classical bust or group of figures where the background is free from flaw, the colours even, and where the curve of the shell has been used to the advantage of the design by the carver. Signed Victorian cameos are not common. Should a good unmounted cameo be found it will be well worth having remounted. Some of the best cameos are found in superbly worked gold mounts, the work of English goldsmiths. Some cameo work was also done by British shell carvers, although very few approached the artistic skills of the Neapolitans. Among the most interesting examples are the commemorative historical subjects cut on small shells recalling such victories as Trafalgar and Waterloo.

Cameos may also be found carved in coral, another material dear to the hearts of the Victorians. It is usually seen in shades of pink and red, but white coral also exists. Coral has increased in price, partly because of its increasing scarcity. Formed by sea creatures, coral has been overharvested by divers and some steps are now being taken to conserve coral stocks. Highly attractive carved coral bracelets, mainly from Italy, were well liked by the Victorians and coral necklaces were popular gifts for babies. Like the coral mounts on babies' silver rattles and whistles, they were perhaps used to aid teething.

Lava cameos are to be found set in rings, brooches and bracelets, and it is in the last setting that they are at their most attractive. Most lava cameos are carved with classical heads cut from shaped tablets of solidified volcanic lava. In colour this volcanic material ranges from dark chocolate and terracotta down to olive and white. The most desirable pieces are those mounted in gold settings but a considerable amount of lava jewellery was also set in silver. Not surprisingly, this carved lava was also known as Pompeian jewellery.

Mosaic jewellery also enjoyed popularity during the mid-19th century. Tiny fragments of coloured glass or marble were assembled and arranged to form views of Rome or classical ruins. A complete matching suite or parure of mosaic jewellery is rarely met with today. Consisting of necklace, brooch, bracelet clasps and ear-rings, it does have a considerable visual impact. Sometimes the pieces bear the word 'Roma'. Florentine mosaics are of an entirely different nature. Instead of a picture built up of chippings, they consist of carefully chosen stones of fine colour, such as red cornelian and the green of malachite. These stones are cut into shape, usually of flowers or birds, and fitted flush into a black background and set in gold or pinchbeck. These are desirable objects frequently overlooked, and are most often found as brooches. Florentine mosaics were also imported into Britain in a far larger form as tops for occasional tables and sometimes in grander forms.

Amber, beleek, and cairngorms

Another fossil material of particular charm is amber, a fossil resin from prehistoric trees. It was a material that had attracted the attention of very early writers with a scientific or magical bent.

Most carved shell cameos of the 19th century were set in gold or silver mounts, while others were admired in cabinets as collector's items. The bracelet is carved in high relief from coloured lava

RIGHT The art of the mosaicist has long flourished in Italy and is still much admired with the result that prices are rising

BELOW Fine agates and the smokey quartz of the Cairngorms have produced a form of folk jewellery of great charm. The black wooden cross is of Irish bog oak and the necklace and hair-comb are of amber.

RIGHT Early 19th-century cast-iron jewellery from Berlin is no longer easy to find but occasionally it is to be found unrecognised on a market stall. The brooch and ear-rings are of tortoise-shell inlaid with gold

The property of amber which so intrigued them was its capacity, when rubbed, to become charged with electricity. This interest was heightened still further by the discovery that much amber contains petrified plant and insect remains. Amber may be opaque or transparent and is extremely light in weight. In colour, amber may range from straw to a dark red. Because of its lightness it was very much favoured for necklaces, and large beads of amber could be used.

Black bog oak from the peat bogs of Ireland, as well as being used for inlay in furniture, was also mounted and inlaid with gold and some fine brooches were produced. Some bog-oak brooches are also set with Irish pearls.

Beleek porcelain from County Fermanagh was also manufactured in the form of brooches. Their beautiful lustre remains and they are well worth searching for.

The Victorian Royal Family itself influenced what may well be termed folk jewellery from Scotland. In 1848 Queen Victoria's love of the Highlands led her to acquire an old house at Balmoral in Aberdeenshire. Prince Albert pulled down the original and erected a castle in the Scottish baronial style. Highland dress and tartan carpets and curtains became the rage and Highland mania was rampant throughout Britain. Scotch pebble brooches abounded, and the agate jewellery mainly mounted in silver of traditional design is still very popular today. Pearls from Scotland's rivers were mounted in company with Scotch pebbles; the delightful smoke quartz of the Cairngorms was highly prized and the larger stones were set in splendid brooches.

Berlin iron jewellery

During the Prussian War with Napoleon (1813–15) money for weapons and for the army was desperately short. In a mood of patriotic fervour people were exhorted to exchange their gold jewellery for copies of it made in iron. Following the final defeat of Napoleon at Waterloo in 1815 the Prussians wore their iron jewellery with pride. This exceptional cast jewellery had been made at the Royal Iron foundry in Berlin since 1804, a secondary product to the main output for heavy industry. Most of the designs were executed in a fine Gothic tracery and much of it was exported throughout Europe. It would almost certainly have been worn by many women as mourning jewellery. Berlin iron jewellery was exhibited in the Great Exhibition in 1851 but it was not long before interest in iron jewellery began to decline. Many pieces were no doubt simply discarded later because they were not made from precious metals; moreover, the fine cast iron tended to be brittle and was quite easily damaged. Now these iron pieces are again sought after, full of history as they are. Occasionally a piece will appear in an antique shop or among bric-a-brac on some market stall, unrecognized by most people.

Pinchbeck, paste, cut steel, ancient and ethnic jewellery

Christopher Pinchbeck (1670–1732) was a watch and clockmaker in Fleet Street, London. It was he who invented an alloy of copper and zinc that produced a metal of a rich yellow closely resembling gold. The alloy was named after its inventor, and was used in the production of such small objects as *etuis* and other *bijouterie* as well as jewellery. When lower gold qualities became legally accepted in Britain, the use of pinchbeck was no longer popular; in fact the term began to be applied to anything that was cheaply gilded or false. Good pinchbeck was well fashioned and is interesting in its own right and is often recognized by its colour.

Paste jewellery has also come into its own once more. Paste means glass that has been used to resemble gem stones; as long ago as the 17th century it was discovered that lead oxide added to glass created glittering reflective surfaces when cut. Whole suites of jewellery were created in paste and were widely worn in society. Foil backing also helped the reflective quality and in the 18th century the finest maker of paste was considered to be Josef Strass.

Cut steel was invented by Matthew Boulton at his great Soho Works, in Birmingham, and later it was also manufactured in Paris. By cutting and polishing the steel as though it were gem stone, much of the appearance and effect of diamonds was remarkably achieved. From the 1760s, for a hundred years, cut steel was used for all manner of decoration, from sword hilts to snuff boxes, but in the field of jewellery it was outstanding. Today, fine pieces may still be obtained at most reasonable prices.

Surprising though it may seem, early Egyptian necklaces formed of glazed clay beads are not hard to find, neither are the simple glass bangles of the Roman period; all of which may be purchased for very modest sums. Collectors are now giving increasing attention to ancient and ethnic jewellery. While jewellery of precious metal continues to rise in value, the bronze rings, brooches, and the colourful semi-precious jewellery of nomadic peoples from the Arabian Desert to the high plateau of Tibet, have opened up a whole new field of study and delight.

ABOVE A fine collection of Victorian rings including, in the top row, an enamelled mourning ring, a mizpah ring, and another mourning ring set with human hair

OPPOSITE TOP RIGHT Pinchbeck is found in the lower price range of Victorian jewellery

OPPOSITE CENTRE LEFT Fine French paste can simulate the fire of diamonds, but it should be regarded as jewellery in its own right

OPPOSITE CENTRE RIGHT Cut steel jewellery has tended to be overlooked in recent years inspite of its craftsmanship which these pieces show well. The floral brooch illustrated here is set *en-tremblant,* meaning since the head of the flower is attached to a spring it trembles when the wearer moves!

OPPOSITE BELOW Early Egyptian pottery bead necklaces and Roman glass bracelets are not difficult to find and may be purchased for a modest sum

Rings

THE GOLD WEDDING RING as such dates from the Reformation when the giving of a ring became part of the wedding ceremony, but very few gold wedding rings of a date before 1800 are found today.

KEEPER RINGS were popular with the Victorians. These were heavy gold rings worn with the wedding ring and usually heavily chased with leaf designs, ivy being a particular favourite. These rings were frequently regarded as a form of portable wealth.

SIGNET RINGS were invariably heavy gold rings with a flat table carrying a device or inscription for impressing the mark of the owner on sealing wax. In medieval times they were regarded as a symbol of authority granted only to a few. Such rings were considered a means of identity and safe passage for those who wore them.

INITIAL RINGS are so called when the initial letters of precious or semi-precious stones are used to spell out a word of affection or the owner's name. Old rings of this type are now costly and difficult to find.

MIZPAH RINGS are still obtainable and were very popular with the Victorians who prized them highly. Made of gold and with the word MIZPAH either engraved or cast in relief they particularly appealed to Victorian sentiment. MIZPAH denotes the occasion when Jacob and his brethren built a cairn of stones at Mizpah of Gilead, and Laban said to Jacob, 'The Lord watch between me and thee, when we are absent one from another.' Victorian brooches in gold, silver and other materials are also found bearing the word Mizpah.

POSY RINGS The word posy is simply an abbreviated form of 'poesy' which may be defined as a brief poetical sentiment. These rings have a line, or lines, of verse or sentiment engraved on the inside of the ring, for example, 'Like this my love shall endless prove.' Early rings of this nature are rare but later examples are to be found from time to time. The custom of inscribing a posy or a motto on brooches survived late into the 19th century in Scotland, where they were given as love tokens. Posy rings were mostly given on St Valentine's Day; usually of gold. When Lady Cathcart married her fourth husband in 1713, she had inscribed on her ring, 'If I survive I will have five.'

WARTIME WEDDING RINGS At the beginning of 1942 the Board of Trade instituted a standard wartime wedding ring in 9-carat gold. These rings are easily distinguished from other 9-carat gold wedding rings because those made during the war carried an additional mark stamped by the Assay Offices, consisting of two intersecting circles within a rectangle. The rings were limited in weight and entirely plain, no ornament of any kind being permitted. It seems very likely that many of these rings would have been replaced after the war, although many women will have retained their original rings and regarded them highly. Historically the wartime wedding ring is important and is worthy of a place among any collection of rings. It should be remembered that while given a special mark by the Assay Offices it is not a hallmark in the strict sense.

BIRTHSTONE RINGS For thousands of years there has existed the belief that gemstones have mystical powers. In turn, gems have been linked with the passage of the sun and the seasons of the year. From here it is but a short step to the signs of the zodiac and the month in which an individual is born. Searching for an antique ring with one's own birthstone is a pleasant activity.

Although there is now far more uniformity on the subject among the jewellers of the world, it is still possible to find variations in stones named for each month, and alternative stones have also been named since the 18th century. Colour has largely determined the stones chosen. In the medieval period it was largely by colour that gemstones were identified which meant that many stones regarded as jewels were not really gemstones at all; the famous Black Prince's ruby to be seen in the State Crown is, in fact, not a ruby but a less valuable spinel. Below is a list of months, stones and colours which may be taken as a guide, although by no means a definitive one.

January Garnet *Dark Red*
February Amethyst *Purple*
March Aquamarine *Pale Blue*
April Diamonds or Rock Crystal *White*
May Emerald *Green*
June Pearl or moonstone *Cream*
July Ruby or Cornelian *Red*
August Peridot or Sardonyx *Pale Green*
September Sapphire or Lapis Lazuli *Deep Blue*
October Opal *Variegated*
November Topaz *Yellow*
December Turquoise *Sky Blue*

A superstition frequently reiterated is that opals are unlucky to all except those born in October. The reason for such stories may well have developed from the fact that opals are easily damaged, and wear may cause colour changes.

Coins and tokens

Coins and historic medallions have long been appreciated by collectors, many of them being considerable works of art in their own right, and all of them representing a facet of history. Who, on finding a silver coin of the reign of George II, marked with the name LIMA, would be anything but fascinated to discover that the silver used in its making had come from captured treasure. The English privateers, the *Duke* and the *Prince Frederick*, had taken two armed French ships in the North Atlantic and, on their return to Britain, the captured silver was immediately taken to the Tower of London where it probably supplied more than half the coinage of George II's reign. Coins of this period, particularly the low denominations, are by no means overpriced. It is also surprising to note the prices obtained for silver coins of the 13th and 14th centuries. A silver penny of the reign of King Edward I, for example, may still be purchased for well under fifty pounds; yet such a coin is in fact a medieval royal portrait that has been actually hammered individually by hand.

Trade tokens

On two occasions in England the lack of small change and the failure of government to deal with the situation, led to the private issues of tokens which were used widely, although they were an illegal form of coinage. The issues were made during the second half of the 17th century, the later 18th and the early 19th centuries. The tokens did not bear the Sovereign's head, but carried instead the name of the tradesman issuing the token, the value it represented and usually a symbol or sign of the trade pursued. Not only were tradesmen involved, but inn-keepers and some town mayors used them too. These tokens were a vital part of local trade, particularly among the poor in meeting their day-to-day needs. These are always well collected but are by no means in short supply and excellent collections can be formed to illuminate local history.

LEFT Shakespeare medal by Dorothy Dick, 1916; Jenny Lind birthday medal by Allen & Moore, 1847; Gertrude Elliott as Cleopatra, medal by R. Tait McKenzie, U.S.A., 1906

BELOW LEFT 17th- and 18th-century trade tokens: *(top)* Thomas Spatehurst, Hosier – his halfpenny; Queen Elizabeth I, portrait of the obverse of the Chichester halfpenny, 1794; mail-coach halfpenny of J. Palmer of Bath, 1797

BELOW RIGHT The bronze portrait medallion depicts Sir Joseph Banks (1743–1820), *(below)* a plated agricultural medal, *c.* 1905; ribboned medals of the Coronations of 1911 and 1937

Hop tokens

Tokens were used in the hop gardens of Britain for more than two centuries. They were used as tallies, enabling a farmer to check the number of bushels of hops picked by individual pickers. According to the quantity of bushels so each picker was paid, exchanging his tokens for coin of the realm at the current rate being paid during that season.

A good deal of what is known of hop tokens has emanated from the writings of the Rev. R. W. H. Acworth who appears to have been the first collector to take a deep interest in the subject some fifty years ago, and it is clear that this is an area where there still remains a great deal of research to be done.

Hop tokens appear to run in values of 1, 3, 6, 12, 30 and 60 bushels. Tokens of 120-bushel value are to be found but these would seem to be somewhat rare. The majority of tokens are cast in lead, while others have been stamped without regard to design or quality. However, quality may also be very high and a good example of this may be seen in the illustration of a 1-bushel token from the Northiam hop garden of J. Winser Lord of 1883. This is a token considerably smaller than the current $\frac{1}{2}$ pence coin, yet it has been cast so well that it has something of the care and charm of an ancient greek silver coin.

Triangular and square tokens were made, and some circular tokens have holes through them in order that they might be safely secured on string. Other metals beside lead were used in token production; zinc, pewter, bronze, copper, brass and tinned iron were all used. Some tokens were made on the farms, others by local craftsmen who would design and manufacture for hop gardens in their areas. Machine-made examples were also supplied to the hopping industry by S. A. Daniell of Birmingham.

Hop tokens were exchanged for cash but were used as a form of currency among the itinerant hop pickers working in the gardens, and the shops and public houses of the nearby villages would also have accepted them for goods. The farmers' price to the picker for the picked bushel being well-known in all hop-growing areas each season.

Billies and Charlies

These most interesting objects are in fact forgeries, but they are well worthy of the attention already given them by many collectors; they might well be described as a genuine form of folk art. This, no doubt, accounts for the curious charm they certainly possess and the affection they tend to evoke.

Although popularly known as 'Billies and Charlies' they may also be described as 'Shadwell Dock Forgeries'. When excavations were being made for a new dock on the Thames at Shadwell between 1857 and 1858 many hundreds of objects of apparent antiquity were discovered in the mud. Later they were found to have been made about twelve years before by two illiterate labourers who played on the universal gullibility of people looking into holes or raking about in mud.

Similar objects continued to be made by the two men known as Billy and Charley, otherwise William Smith and Charles Eaton, who lived in Rosemary Lane on Tower Hill. They manufactured medallions, vases and figures of all kinds and these have now become very widely distributed. The majority of these pieces are made either from lead or from a poor quality pewter known as 'cock metal'.

It was the intention of Billy and Charley that

BELOW A group of lead hop tokens, from Kent and Sussex, ranging in denomination from 1–60 bushels and a 19th century Rye pottery jar

BELOW RIGHT A typical example of the work of Billie and Charlie

their products should be passed off as objects of medieval antiquity and, indeed, many were and, come to that, still are.

These medallions or pendants frequently resemble horse brasses in form and size, having busts in low relief surrounded by fake inscriptions and arabic numerals. They are still excavated from time to time today and the practised eye will almost certainly recognize them at once for what they are. Many examples disastrously mix the periods of costume, armour and lettering.

Most of the objects made by this ingenious pair of illiterates were inspired by medieval pilgrims' badges or souvenirs, originally manufactured for the faithful who were visiting such shrines as St Thomas Becket at Canterbury or that of St Richard at Chichester.

William Smith and Charles Eaton began producing their 'antiquities' after finding a genuine pilgrim's badge and, having sold it to the Bristol Museum, decided that with a little self-help further profits were to be made. Inscriptions found on their work make no sense at all, and most of the dates appear to range between 1000 and 1030. Even so, two 'Billies and Charlies' did appear in a post-war exhibition of Byzantine Art in the United States!

Cast in chalk moulds and 'aged' with acid, the production of these pieces would have been done when the daily heavy labour was over. It could all have been something of a relaxation for the two labourers as well as a supplement to their wages of 80p per week; and in the process they also achieved a rather strange immortality.

Nuremberg jettons

The role of the early jettons was intended to be as reckoning or casting counters and they were in vogue from the 13th to the 17th centuries. They were used in calculations of all kinds, in the compiling of accounts and the checking of bills. They were, in fact, an attractive and vital part of commercial activity from England to Italy. Their use first developed in France and it was the clink of the brass jetton rather than gold itself that was the familiar sound in the counting-houses of merchants and noblemen.

Although jettons were made in many parts of Europe, it was the city of Nuremberg that became the main production centre, particularly from the 16th century, and it is these that are most commonly found today.

Jettons were used in conjunction with a counter table, or a counter board, surfaces that were often covered with a felt reckoning cloth or carpet marked out with lines for calculation. The regular lines that formed squares on these cloths explains the derivation of 'Exchequer'.

The cloths, and sometimes the tables or boards themselves, had lines that represented increasing values, the first line being 1, the second 10, the third 100, the fourth 1000 and so on. In the same way a jetton laid between any two lines would indicate a sum of half the larger figure. It was a simple and ingenious method of computation that permitted the management of large figures and their addition and subtraction to be handled with great ease.

When such accounting methods were discarded early in the 18th century, the jetton was relegated to the gaming table until counters or 'chips' were manufactured for that specific use. Even so, jettons must have been used as money from time to time in daily transactions during periods when small change was scarce.

For the collector, jettons provide an opportunity to open new fields of interest at a remarkably modest cost. Increasing interest is being shown in the English medieval tokens but the majority of Nuremberg tokens cost but little. The ordinary stock jetton that was manufactured in very large numbers at Nuremberg is easily obtained and provides an ideal introduction to the subject for the beginner. Through such pieces an awareness will soon develop of the wide range of jettons that are to be searched out, some of them very fine indeed.

The stock jetton is easily recognized with its decorative patterns of crowns and fleurs-de-lis on the obverse and the *Reichsapfel* or crowned orb of Nuremberg on the reverse. These jettons are found in two sizes that correspond roughly with the old penny and halfpenny size of British currency. Other patterns include ships of various design, scenes of classical mythology, a whole range of Biblical subjects, and some that provide town views, historical scenes, and others of political interest.

Jettons that most enthusiasts try to obtain are those that portray a *Rechenmeister* in his Tudor period dress at his counting table, together with money bags and jettons. They also have an incomplete alphabet on the reverse and some are dated. A number of variations of this jetton exist.

ABOVE *Rechenmeister* jetton showing a man seated at a counting table with a money bag, eleven jettons and a book, Nuremberg, *c.* 1550

TOP A group of five jettons: *(top left to bottom right)* King Edward III standing under a canopy, *c.* 1350; the so-called Black Death jetton, France, 1347–9; French ship jetton, made in Nuremberg, 16th century; Nuremberg jetton, depicting the lion of St Mark, 16th century; Tournai jetton of the Dauphin, 15th century

Jettons by Hans Schultes, Krauwinckle and Wolf Laufer, 16th and 17th century

Such an example costs from £15 to £40 according to condition.

Jetton manufacture in Nuremberg appears to have been very much in the hands of a few manufacturing families who would have employed a considerable workforce. Many of the jettons bear the maker's name or his initials and the name Nuremberg may also be present.

This is a subject that has much to offer and, like all worthwhile interests, the beginner will do well to buy from experienced coin dealers, who have a recognized reputation, and to study the various books and numismatic publications that treat jettons from time to time.

Among some of the more important Nuremberg manufacturers who supplied jettons that were widely used in Britain, and whose activities ranged over a period *circa* 1550–1650, are the following: George Schultes, Hans Schultes, Kilianus Koch, Wolf Laufer, Hans Laufer, Matheus Laufer, Conrad Laufer, Damianus Krauwinckel, Egidius Krauwinckel, Hans Krauwinckel (the most prolific of the Nuremberg jetton makers), Zacharius Jansen, and Valentinus Maler.

It is worth noting that the counter table is among the rarest examples of early English furniture. They are mentioned in Chaucer as well as in many early inventories. The Victoria and Albert Museum has two late examples from the 16th century, and a few others are in private hands. Early 'reckoning cloths' are also very rare, but the Bayerisches National Museum in Munich has five examples.

A Thomas Becket pilgrim badge having a particularly fine patination, late 15th century. Such a badge, frequently worn on one's hat, was recently recovered from the Thames at Billingsgate, London

Pilgrim badges

This is, again, an area not as widely prospected among collectors as it deserves to be. Pilgrim badges provide an opportunity to acquire an attractive series of medieval works of art in lead or pewter that have a fascinating story to tell.

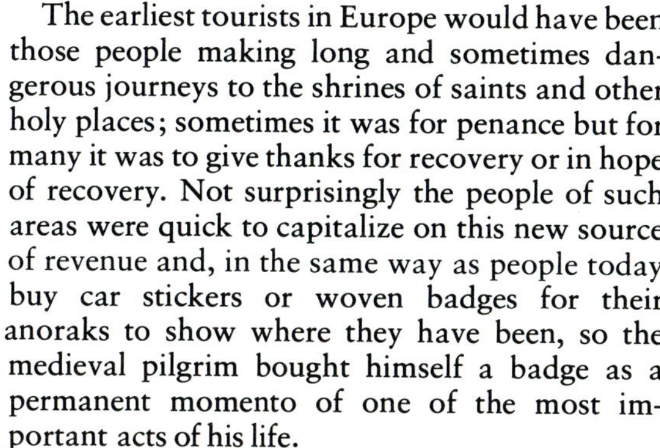

The earliest tourists in Europe would have been those people making long and sometimes dangerous journeys to the shrines of saints and other holy places; sometimes it was for penance but for many it was to give thanks for recovery or in hope of recovery. Not surprisingly the people of such areas were quick to capitalize on this new source of revenue and, in the same way as people today buy car stickers or woven badges for their anoraks to show where they have been, so the medieval pilgrim bought himself a badge as a permanent momento of one of the most important acts of his life.

In Britain the most popular shrine was that of Becket at Canterbury and there was another at London Bridge. Geoffrey Chaucer described pilgrimages in his *Canterbury Tales*. Later, in the *Vision Of Piers Plowman* by Langland, the pilgrim draws attention to the badges he has obtained from the shrines he has visited in the words:

Ye may se by my signes
That sitten on myn hatte.

Most of the badges were either made so that they might be sewn or pinned on to clothing, or suspended from the neck in the manner of a pendant. The designs of such pieces are diverse and often most attractive. An arm and hand in the act of blessing denotes St Richard. Many single letters are to be found denoting the name of a saint, for example, a 'W' for our Lady of Walsingham, or a 'T' for St Thomas of Canterbury, and are sometimes set within a circular border or in a quatrefoil. The scallop shell denoting St James of Compostella is well known, and many badges took the form of small flasks known as ampullae. It had been the custom to place a drop of the blood of St Thomas of Canterbury, much diluted with water, into these leaden flasks for pilgrims; but it is very doubtful if any of the actual blood of the martyr would really have been used for this purpose.

Large numbers of pilgrim badges have been recovered from mud banks and river beds, and particularly from the Thames and the Seine. Certain of the badges are highly pictorial with a definite narrative quality. A few of the original stone moulds have been found from which these badges were cast. A fine example is the mould for casting equestrian figures of St Thomas of Canterbury, and now in the British Museum. Most of the pilgrim badges date from the 13th, 14th and 15th centuries. Later badges of polished metal and engraved with figures of popular saints are sometimes seen, but these are more likely to be personal amulets worn for protection, rather than a true pilgrim badge.

The figure of St Barbara also appears to have been in popular demand during the late Middle Ages as she was regarded as a guardian against sudden death – much as the motorist of today tends to carry a figure of St Christopher attached to his car keys.

Toys and dolls

From the 17th century to 1914 the most prominent nation in terms of toymaking was Germany. The toys were mainly of wood until the 19th century when tin-plate mechanical toys entered the arena. Many of the old German toys are to be found in all parts of the Western world. Indeed, the appeal of collecting toys and dolls would now appear to be universal.

For the Germans, toymaking rapidly became a major industry employing thousands of people. Wooden figure models were made in one piece out of wood and some were given jointed bodies. Detail is certainly neglected among the early wooden toys but the charm of the coaches and horses and the trains of the 1840s and fifties is undeniable. The later ships and aircraft belong to a make-believe world rather than setting out faithfully to reproduce new methods of transport and propulsion. During the 19th century the most favoured nursery toy was the Noah's Ark. Some were painted, others left plain, and most of them originated in Bavaria. Noah's Ark was very much a toy for use on a Sunday, when ball games or hoops would have been quite out of the question. Most arks were fitted with opening side sections so that the pairs of carved wood animals and Mr and Mrs Noah could easily be moved in and out. Toy arks were even made by French prisoners using wood and straw while held in Britain during the Napoleonic Wars.

Cock-horses and rocking horses were always popular, although old examples are no longer easy to find. Those that are found, frequently require skilful and sympathetic restoration. Tin-plate toys began to make great inroads into the toy market during the 1860s. Germany continued leader in the field, although France and other European countries were realizing the potential market and toymaking began to boom. In due course Britain and America were themselves able to export to the Continent, although both nations had been supplying their home markets for many years. These cheap tin-plate toys are now pursued by thousands of enthusiasts. Some examples take the form of simple automata in which the turning of wheels set knife-grinders to work and oarsmen rowing. Cast-iron toys had already pioneered the field with mechanical money boxes, William Tell shooting a coin from his crossbow, or a black figure popping coins into his open mouth as soon as they were placed in his hand.

The firm of Ernst Paul Lehmann made many of the tin-plate clockwork toys in Germany from 1881. His toys are marked either with the word 'Lehmann' or the initials 'EPL'. Another important maker was the Frenchman Fernand Martin, a manufacturer who, between 1878 and 1912, had an output of three-quarters of a million high quality mechanical toys a year. In the early years of this century toys by Martin could be bought for less than 10p.

Buffalo Bill, Mickey Mouse, Goofy and Donald Duck, and Charlie Chaplin are all highly prized as mechanical toys. The rare automata that include dancing figures, acrobats, musicians, and dancing bears from the firm of Decamps, are the high-water mark of mechanical toy production. Such automata are now beyond the reach of most of us, but a group of wooden toys made by the Japanese and known as Kobi toys are still reasonably acquired. They all have moving parts and, although the figures are somewhat grotesque, they are imaginative and well made.

Among makers the names to note of clockwork toys are the following: Gunthermann, Bing, Hess, Marklin, Georges Carette, Rossignal and Schreyer. All tin-plate toys that have painted advertisements are in demand, as are the cast Dinky toys of the 20th century. Toys in their original boxes attract special attention, so do the products of Chad Valley, Tootsie Toys and Wells-Brimtoy.

Toy soldiers were carved from wood and made in tin in the 19th century, but William Britain working in London began the hollow casting of

Two Lehmann toys. *Li-la and the auto-sisters* was issued 1900–1904. The dog tries to get away from the sisters who try hard to beat him. *Oh-my* tap dances on his tin base and was issued from World War I until the 1930s

lead soldiers in 1893 which stimulated an astonishing demand. Though not antiques, lead soldiers appear regularly in major collectors' sales, and the British lead soldiers made prior to 1914 are regarded as of the greatest importance by collectors. Adult interest in toy soldiers continues to grow as collections are built up of favourite regiments. War games have created more collectors.

It was not until several years after World War I, that people began collecting dolls. Now the dolls of the 18th century have become rarities and the main focus is on the dolls of the 19th and 20th centuries. As with most examples of juvenilia, collecting dolls is by no means a cheap hobby. The mass-producted German pegwooden dolls, sometimes called Dutch dolls, were well made and painted in spite of their large numbers. They are still to be found in reasonable numbers and condition and the majority of them range in size from 15cm to 2.5cm (6in to 1in). The pegwoodens were very popular from 1830, and it was also a period when German play dolls with papier-mâché heads enjoyed considerable popularity.

Ten years later papier-mâché-headed dolls that had been dipped in wax were introduced. Features were painted and hair was glued on. Few of these are found today in reasonable condition.

RIGHT Box of soldiers by Britain, 1890s; *(below left)* an original tin soldier, French, 1910

BELOW *(back row)* Large celluloid doll (Japanese); Land Army girl (Chad Valley Co. Ltd); a wax doll with a rag body; *(front row)* parian German dolls; baby doll, French; American doll (Alexander Doll Co.)

All china-headed dolls of the first half of the 19th century are of interest. Early examples made between 1825 and 1850 are known as *Biedermeier.* The heads have a black spot on an otherwise bald pate, which some authorities believe may have been a mark to indicate where a wig might be fastened.

Bisque china heads, so called because they were unglazed, were made from 1850. Some heads were sold separately with the intention that the bodies could be made up and dressed at home, but they are very often completely out of proportion.

Bisque must not be confused with the Parian heads used on dolls of the same period. Although Parian ware was an English development, also known as 'statuary porcelain', it is difficult to differentiate between those made in England and those from the Continent. Parian very much resembles marble in texture. China-headed dolls of all types may often be dated from the detail of their moulded hair styles.

Some dolls' heads were made at Dresden and bear the crossed swords mark of the factory in underglaze blue. Dolls that have impressed proper names will belong to the end of the century, as will all those with simulated jewellery embedded in them. Brown-eyed dolls are rare in comparison with those of blue. Much later German china-headed dolls will have a number, name or set of initials somewhere on the head, neck or shoulder that will enable the manufacturer and period to be identified.

Between 1850 and 1860 some excellent wax dolls were made in London. They were produced by pouring hot wax into moulds. Fitted with glass eyes, and with real hair and eyebrows pricked into position they are highly attractive. These dolls were, and remain, expensive products and it was not until the end of the century that fine dolls, mostly German, were being offered at a price the public at large could afford.

Pedlar dolls date from the first half of the 19th century and are of English make and usually manufactured in wood. Wearing a cloak, bonnet, and a print dress, these figures carry a basket or tray containing wares of all kinds. These dolls are rare and seldom found in anything approaching original condition.

French fashion dolls are scarce and highly prized. They have bisque heads with soft complexions, and are beautifully worked throughout, the bodies strongly stitched in order that clothes might be easily changed. Most fashion dolls have heads that swivel, and the ears are pierced so that ear-rings may be worn. Many modern copies of fashion dolls exist, so caution needs to be exercised when buying.

There is a wide range of American dolls of great interest, together with dolls made of many different materials, from rubber to celluloid. Collectors of all dolls would be well advised to consult the major reference works on the subject, some of which are listed on page 79.

Metalwork

Brass and copper

Brass and copper have been used to manufacture household objects for centuries, both metals reflecting warmth and glow when polished. The affection in which brass and copper has always been held is demonstrated by the reproduction items produced in their tens of thousands. Helmet-shaped coal scuttles, brass and copper warming pans, copper kettles and other fakes abound. While books may be consulted there really is no substitute for handling original items in order to make comparisons with copies and fakes. A copy is precisely that, although most so-called 'copies' are but loosely based on originals; on the other hand, a fake is made with care in order to be passed off as an original and is therefore a far more dangerous proposition.

◩ BRASS WARMING PANS date from 1400, and the pans were made from Dutch brass. It was once the custom of a servant to be sent to bed in order to warm the master's sheets, a pastime less

The copper cone-shaped receptacle in the left foreground is for heating or 'mulling' ale. The Britannia metal coffee pot is an example of a material that now attracts increasing attention

dangerous, perhaps, than using a bed warmer; for it is clear from a study of early household inventories that many beds were destroyed by fire.

Copper warming pans became popular during the 18th century and were manufactured in company with brass pans well into the reign of Queen Victoria. Many of the original turned wood handles became affected by woodworm, so it is not uncommon today to find an old pan with a replacement handle.

◪ CANDLESTICKS of the late 18th and the 19th centuries are still to be obtained from markets and antique shops without too much difficulty. From about 1770 the demand for candlesticks increased as they became cheaper due to improvements in casting. Stem and socket were cast in a single piece, then applied to a cast foot. In the 18th century candlesticks tended to follow the current neo-classical silver shapes, but the Victorian candlesticks seldom possess the same sense of character. Victorian brass chamber candlesticks are well worth obtaining, as are the brass hot-water cans that were produced in a whole range of sizes.

◪ COPPER ALE WARMERS are found in various shapes and sizes but the most popular are those of shoe or conical shape. They were thrust into the embers to prepare a welcome drink for a cold winters' night!

◪ BRASS FENDERS 18th-century brass fenders are very small in comparison with those of the following century. The comfortable Victorian fender with its brass fire irons became standard furnishing in the Victorian home. In the 18th century fire irons were made of polished steel, but the brass shovel, poker and tongs of the 19th century are as popular as ever today. Copper coal scoops and brass helmet-shaped coal scuttles, together with the early circular trivets or later rectangular examples, completed the glittering scene. Some trivets were made to clip on to the firebars of the grate. Large heavy trivets on four legs with handles, or a slot in the top to provide a grip, are known as footmen. Set in a small room, a brass footman becomes an important part of the furnishings.

◪ BRASS LAMPS with paraffin oil being used as fuel, outshone all other lamps. These lamps with the tall glass chimneys and brass oil reservoirs were a feature of many houses until 1945. Once discarded in favour of gas or electric light, they are again much prized.

◪ OTHER ITEMS Brass chestnut roasters, clockwork brass bottle jacks for turning the roast joint, shaped copper stomach warmers, and large copper containers for warming the feet while on long train journeys, are but part of the panorama of copper and brass open to the collector.

The gleam of brass and copper in the hearth has always been an attraction. Note the three-legged skillet and the chestnut roaster in the foreground

A pewter mug, *c.* 1860, together with a pair of art nouveau 'Tudric' pewter vases, early 20th century

Pewter

Pewter has long been a favourite with collectors, but early pewter is now rare. Pewter is an alloy consisting of tin with the addition of lead or copper, sometimes both. Antimony and bismuth have also been added to the formula from time to time. Various qualities of pewter were produced but the recognition of these are only acquired through knowledge and experience. The beginner should first bear in mind that the darker the pewter the more lead it is likely to contain, the more silver grey the greater the tin content. The Pewterers' Company required of their members by statute that their manufactures should be marked with what are known as 'touch marks' denoting the maker. Some fine pewter of the late 17th and early 18th centuries actually carries fraudulent silver hallmarks, so beware!

Pewter spoons, bowls, candlesticks, mugs, plates, salts, hot-water plates, and measures form fine collections, and the regional types associated with the Channel Islands, Scotland, Wales and Ireland are of great interest. It is still possible to come upon early pewter while searching for 19th-century pieces, so once again the collector should study his subject carefully if the 'special piece' is to be recognized. Art nouveau pewter is well worth serious consideration. Ignored for fifty years its quality is again being appreciated and is now much in demand. One of the most important of the pewter factories working in Germany was that of J. P. Kayser Sohn. Sold under the trade name '*Kayserzinn*' many of this firm's lines were marketed in London by Arthur Lasenby Liberty from his famous shop in Regent Street.

Liberty revelled in the more restrained forms of Art Nouveau and he imported pewter from a number of German factories. British pewter had fallen to a low ebb and Liberty was quick to realize that '. . . the Germans have recently produced many original and pleasing designs in pewter'. So in 1903 he began the production of English-made pewter, calling it 'Tudric' ware. Some of the early pieces of 'Tudric' were designed by Reginald Silver (1879–1965) and Archibald Knox (1864–1933). Good representative pieces of 'Tudric' made during the early years of the century should be purchased where possible, for it is unlikely they will be overlooked again.

Britannia metal

Britannia metal is an alloy of tin and antimony and objects made of this metal have been looked upon with derision until very recent years. An unprejudiced second look revealed that not all was rotten in the state of Britannia metal. A

Sheffield plate has all the charm of old silver with the advantage of sometimes being obtainable at far less cost

product of the Industrial Revolution, early Britannia metal has great charm. Most of it was made in Sheffield and the makers stamped their names intaglio into the bases of the objects they made. The silver shapes of the day were carefully followed. Makers to look out for are J. Dixon & Son, P. Ashberry, Broadhead and Atkins, James Vickers and James Wolstenholme. Do not confuse pieces marked E.P.B.M. (Electro-Plated Britannia Metal) with the pieces under discussion here. After 1850 the standard of design falls away disastrously. In the words of the 19th-century politician John Bright, 'Silence is golden, speech is silver, but to say one thing and mean another is Britannia metal.'

Sheffield plate

Sheffield plate was the discovery of a Sheffield cutler in the 1740s named Thomas Bolsover. He found that a sheet of copper and a sheet of silver rolled together under heat and pressure caused them to fuse in a double layer that could be worked as though it were one. Unlike many discoverers he realized exactly what he had found, the possibilities of the material and the opportunity of commercial success. In the same way that the furniture designs of Thomas Chippendale were to put good design within the reach of craftsmen and estate carpenters, Sheffield plate put silver on to the tables of people who could not otherwise have afforded such luxury. It was all part of a great social revolution.

Sheffield plate flourished and it was not many years before it was being made by Matthew Boulton in Birmingham. All kinds of objects were made, from buttons to snuff-boxes, coffee pots, candlesticks and urns. Sheffield plate provides a most worthy field for the collector and puts 18th-century objects well within reach. It was the discovery of nickel silver and the later development of electroplate that was to cause the downfall of Sheffield plate. The process of electroplate deposits a mere 'film' of silver on to a base metal body, unlike the layer of metal used in Sheffield plate; this can help the collector to make positive identification where the edges of Sheffield plate can be examined. Silver or heavily plated copper is sometimes used to conceal joints or edges. Sheffield plate should be washed rather than polished, and any cleaning that is required should be carried out with great care. Silver is a soft metal and too much wear will soon reveal the copper beneath. Should worn Sheffield plate items be obtained it is unwise to have them re-plated by electrolysis, as this can only destroy the antique interest of such pieces.

Domestic bygones

Very few of the objects that we describe today as bygones are antiques, but they are of special interest to collectors because of the past way of life they represent. As well as being curious, beautiful, or both, they tell us more graphically than anything else how our ancestors lived. The changes that have occurred since the Coronation of Queen Victoria are unprecedented. In 1837 many households in Britain would have begun the the day by reaching for a tinder box to obtain light and heat by the striking of flint and steel. Conditions of living have now changed beyond recognition, and if change on the land was slower in coming, come it did, with the result that the everyday goods and implements of our grandparents have become laden with nostalgia as well as interest. Some objects are now so far removed from our experience that when we are confronted with them we are no longer able to identify them or their original function. Interest in bygones has advanced rapidly in recent years as more collectors come to realize their interest and the delightful ability that many such pieces have for enhancing the home. The following selection of bygones demonstrates the wide range of objects that it is possible to collect.

KNIFE CLEANERS Popular now as a decorative object and conversation piece the knife cleaner, which was once essential equipment in all butler's pantries, is rarely used today for the purpose for which it was made. Before the general use of stainless steel, however, there was no other satisfactory method of keeping such cutlery clean. Although the drum-type knife cleaner is of a near standard size, 40.7cm (16in) in diameter, the quality of such machines varied greatly. Some examples can still be purchased very cheaply but these are usually very plain pine drums on simple stands and more often than not show severe signs of wear and worm. The cost of such objects

Utensils of the bygone pantry and kitchen, including a knife cleaner *(top left)*, brown-glazed storage jars, butter scoop, pats, and roller, ivory-handled bread knife, sugar cutters, and a wooden-handled copper skimmer

A Victorian box-iron, a stoneware foot warmer, a boot remover, hat irons, a goffering iron, a candle snuffer and a pair of shoe trees

frequently depends upon where they were purchased; for example, a knife cleaner included in the famous auction sale at Mentmore in Buckinghamshire, once the home of the Rothschild family, realized just over £100. In more humble situations knife cleaners of the highest quality should be obtainable at a far lower figure. The cleaner illustrated, a late example, shows signs of Art Nouveau in its iron frame and is fitted with brass and ivory guides for the knives. Surprising though it may seem canisters of the original Wellington knife polish are still to be found.

◪ HORN BEAKERS Most interesting collections of cow-horn beakers can still be formed. The beakers are to be found in a great range of sizes and were made from the horn of a cow. The base of each beaker was carefully fitted and sealed by heat. Cow horn, unlike stag horn, is not a continuation of the skull and if buried for any length of time deteriorates badly. In the 18th and 19th centuries they formed the principal drinking vessels of the cottager and the plain examples still appear regularly in junk shops and on antique-market stalls. The most attractive beakers bear incised and scratched decoration usually rather primitive in technique but depicting rural and farmyard scenes; once again it is not unusual to find the names of individuals and dates incised in this way. Occasionally a rare silver-mounted horn beaker is to be found. These may be dated from the hallmark and the best examples are those from the 18th century, but these are far more costly than their 19th century fellows. Victorian horn beakers with glass bottoms are not uncommon and some horn vessels often believed to be a crude form of beaker are in fact drenches for administering medicine to a sick animal.

◪ STONE JARS Brown stoneware saltglazed storage jars are both practical and look well in any kitchen today. Most jars of this type belong to the second half of the 19th century but unfortunately, like Toby jugs, very few of them are seen with their original loose-fitting lids. The small lug handles at the shoulder of these vessels are a typical feature and many jars have a simple incised decoration around the body.

◪ ROLLING PINS Although modern pins have been made in the same style all early examples have a turned knob at one end only.

◪ BREAD BOARDS 19th-century examples carved with flowers and ears of wheat are among the most interesting. Simple inscriptions are also carved in the borders ranging from 'Bread' to such things as the 'Staff of Life'. While similar wording may be seen on 20th-century boards the Victorian examples are usually found in Gothic lettering.

◪ BREAD KNIVES Victorian high-quality Sheffield-made bread knives are to be found with steel blades, hallmarked silver bolsters and carved bone handles.

◪ BUTTER SCOOPS, PRINTS AND PATS These highly collectable implements of the Victorian and Edwardian kitchen that were found both in cottage and mansion, make very attractive decorations and collections. Butter pats are easily obtained and have either a smooth face or a reeded finish. Although regarded today as a curiosity these objects were very much part of the labour of a dairymaid. The butter pats and prints possess the true sense of folk art and when good examples are found they should not be missed.

◪ PESTLES AND MORTARS Rare early examples are found in bronze, iron, and bell-metal and many mortars have cast inscriptions and dates. Because of their age and rarity they tend to be beyond the means of most collectors, although some good early stone mortars can still be found. Victorian ceramic pestles and mortars were made by various manufactories including Wedgwood.

◪ FLAT IRONS Victorian flat irons, now often used as book ends, played a major part in the life of servants and housewives until well after the World War II. No doubt there are still many women using them today. While most irons are factory produced, some interesting blacksmith-made irons occasionally come to light and are obviously of particular attraction to all collectors of the domestic scene of the past. So too is the heavy box iron with its wooden handle and sliding trapdoor compartment that held the shaped piece of red-hot iron after it was taken from the fire.

◪ LARGE-SIZE CUP AND SAUCERS It is very doubtful if these cups and saucers ever formed part of a service. Such cups are often 10.2cm (4in) high and 11.5cm ($4\frac{1}{4}$in) in diameter with the saucer nearing 20.4cm (8in), with sloping sides. Very much a product of the Victorian age they are usually found in cream earthenware, the better examples bearing Etruscan patterns which were popular with many of the Staffordshire manufacturers in the middle of the century. Breakfast cups can be dated to the 1760s but the very large cups and saucers described here belong to a group entirely on their own. The cups were particularly favoured by the mill workers in the North of England. Miners, also, who came to work in other areas were entitled in their lodgings to a cup of cocoa at night but had to provide their own cups; so the bigger the cup the more cocoa.

◪ GAME PIE DISHES Most of these have decoration in high relief and the best examples are those made during the early 19th century at the Etruria Works of Wedgwood. For many years during the 19th century they were produced in large numbers. Wedgwood examples are invariably stamped with an impressed mark, 'wedgwood'. Unmarked examples are almost certainly the work of other potteries. These are decorative things to have in the kitchen and today they tend to be very popular, yet for a long time they went quite out of favour. They were made in cane ware, a fine pottery with a moulded relief decoration of birds and vines and grapes. The lid of the dish was surmounted by a hare for the handle, surrounded by various game birds. They were made in imitation of pie-crusts during the flour shortage in England at the beginning of the 19th century and so very much reflect social conditions of the time. At the end of the 18th century in a fine country house or farmhouse a traditional game pie would be presented at table with a pastry crust built up to about 12.7cm (5in), literally sculptured and moulded with game birds and similar motifs. It must have looked very grand indeed as it was brought into the dining-room, when the top would have been broken open and the game pie served. The pastry crust itself was not eaten, but later carried out into the kitchen where it was consumed by servants and regarded almost as a staple diet by various wayfarers who came to the kitchen doors of such houses. When pastry became in short supply and therefore expensive, the story is that Wedgwood, with their very excellent commercial vision and artistic eye, provided just the object which would take its place, although it did not help the poor who called at the kitchen for pastry. In the antique trade game pie dishes of this type are often referred to as 'Ceramic Pastry'.

◪ PIN CUSHIONS Good pin cushions are difficult to find though plain examples are easily found. Some of the early 19th-century pin cushions are delightful and often bear various inscriptions and verses worked carefully into them, such as 'Bless the Babe', and 'Spare the Mother'. These were curious gifts but very useful when needles were no doubt working busily to clothe the new arrival. A collection of a dozen or so, framed to be displayed on a wall, look splendid. Pins were fairly scarce in the 18th and 19th centuries and tended to be kept in boxes and little ivory baskets, but the pin cushion became very fashionable during the 19th century, although you but rarely, and excitingly, find a few examples from the earlier century. It is not unusual to see Sheffield plate coasters and even cruet frames diverted from the dining-room and stuffed and padded to take pins.

◪ KNITTING SHEATHS These most interesting curiosities of the past are now much collected by all those interested in the crafts and pastimes of the 18th and 19th centuries. The knitting sheath was used to support one end of a knitting needle, leaving one hand free to deal with the wool. Quite a number of elderly people today continue to knit with one needle clenched beneath one arm. Other people hold the needles one in each hand, and move them with great freedom, but the old way of

ABOVE An oversized cup and saucer, a moustache cup and saucer and a linen polisher

OPPOSITE TOP Spode chamber pot, 1820, and a coloured glaze earthenware spitton, Staffordshire, *c.* 1870

OPPOSITE CENTRE Carved wooden knitting sheath, *c.* 1800

OPPOSITE BELOW Stone bottle muff warmer, a quill cutter, sovereign scales and a silver-plated skirt clip

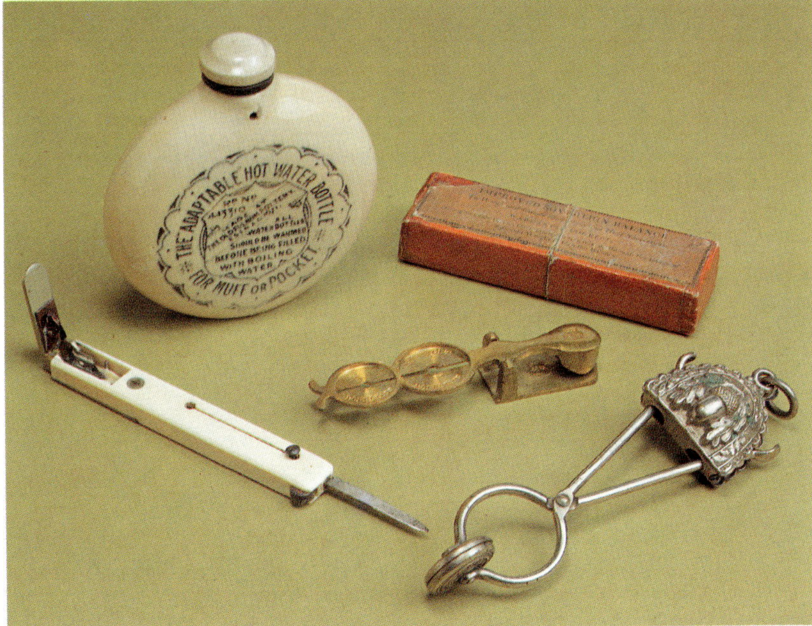

knitting was to have one needle static. The knitting sheath usually takes the form of a wooden stick, but they are to be found in bone, and occasionally from a section of antler. They are mostly about 23cm (9in) long, sometimes rather shorter, with a hole bored in one end, and the other end shaped to fit into the belt. The shaped end is curved to fit the body, slips into the belt and is held still by bringing the arm down on to it. The hole in the top is not a hole bored right through but simply an indentation to take the needle. Very often these were treated as love tokens, with all kinds of suitable decoration and inscriptions carved on them, with the best of them usually bearing the owner's name together with the date. They were used by men as well as women, for men knitted a great deal in the 18th century, particularly shepherds and people who spent a lot of time on their own. These objects are highly decorative, nice to handle, and are a very definite fragment of social history. They are similar in feeling to Welsh love spoons.

■ QUILL CUTTERS are often found with the mark of Mappin Brothers, the registered mark used by this firm on plated goods from 1850. The quill has been used as an instrument for writing for centuries. They are the feathers taken from the wing of a large bird, usually a goose, but feathers from crows, ravens, even turkeys and swans have been used by quill makers. What is essential to the production of a quill is to have a strong feather which has a good tube or barrel portion to it. The end of the barrel portion of the feather was put into the quill cutter, the top of which when pressed down stamped out a section in the form of a nib. In *Pickwick*, Dickens refers to a hard-nibbed pen 'which could be warranted not to splutter' and shaping a quill was always the great problem when cutting quills by hand – if the thickness of the nib was not correct the ink gathered or blotted or spluttered. So, to make things easier, a quill cutter was invented which stamped all the quills to exactly the required dimensions. Many individuals, associations and institutions have used quills well into this century. The British Museum continued to use quills in the reading room well into the Edwardian period and possibly even later than that.

■ SKIRT HOLDERS The last twenty years of the 19th century saw the development of the skirt holder in the form of a miniature pair of tongs hung from the waist by a small chain. It was used to lift a lady's long dress by a few inches in order to keep the material clear of the ground. In many towns and villages at that period streets were still very muddy in winter and dusty in summer. Examples are to be found in brass, plate, silver and other metals.

■ HAND OR MUFF WARMERS come in various forms. Miniature hot-water bottles in stoneware or copper were once common, most of the stoneware examples being made at the Fulham Pottery. Other warmers consisted of an inner container and an outer grill. The container held hot charcoal and supplied heat for a long period, ideal no doubt for long coach or train journeys, not to mention the enduring of the marathon sermons for which certain Victorian clergymen were renowned.

■ LINEN POLISHERS are like wooden darning mushrooms but made of solid glass and used to rub a high finish on starched cottons and linens.

Lead tobacco box, a brass candle extinguisher, a back-scratcher and two pin cushions

◪ SUGAR CUTTERS When sugar was delivered in tall 'welsh-hat' shaped loaves to shops and kitchens, cutters were required to break off the hard loaf sugar. Strongly made of steel, they are to be found unmounted and having the appearance of a sturdy hand tool, or they are mounted on a board for use on a shop counter or kitchen table (see illustration).

◪ CANDLE EXTINGUISHERS Found in silver and Sheffield plate these objects look remarkably like a child's peashooter, the business end of the tube usually flattened into a 'fishtail'. They were used for blowing out bedside candles, low hanging chandeliers and far more often the candelabra set in the middle of a crowded dining table. Although mainly used during the 19th century, silver examples are to be found as late as 1920.

◪ LEAD TOBACCO BOXES Very much favoured by smokers as it was considered that lead kept the tobacco very cool, they were used from the 17th century through the Victorian era. Most of the examples that are found are of a casket shape, rectangular, with widely chamfered corners and a domed lid. The lids frequently have a knob handle in the form of a human head. To be fully complete these boxes have a flat inner 'lid' used to keep the tobacco pressed and moist. The best examples have raised decorations and sometimes bear traces of having been previously painted. It is believed that some of the later examples were manufactured from lead bullets brought back from the Crimea.

◪ WOODEN SNUFF BOXES Treen is the name given to all small wooden collectable objects. The classification is therefore a broad one and it has been suggested that the term might be applied to all wooden objects smaller than a spinning wheel. Wooden snuff boxes are the most pleasing examples of treen, most of them taking the form of shoes, boots, coffins and books. Decorations consist of patterns created by the use of brass-headed tacks or pins. Most desirable are those bearing dates, names or initials.

Wooden snuff boxes of very high craftmanship were also made in Scotland. Some are horn lined and the snuff-proof hinges of these boxes are outstanding examples of the box-maker's skill. Tartan boxes became popular during the second half of the 19th century. Late examples are ornamented with printed scenes on sycamore; some of these boxes are termed Mauchline Ware.

◪ CANDLE SNUFFERS Before the cone-shaped covers were used to extinguish candles, a scissor-like object with two discs was used to pinch the wick of the candle. These objects, known as 'douters' are now rare. Far more commonplace is the snuffer which has a similar scissor action and a pointed end. The purpose of the snuffer was not to extinguish the flame but to service it. With the old fast-burning tallow candles, the wick would curl over and the flame would gutter as it touched the candle fat. To prevent this happening the point of the snuffer was used to raise the wick and the charred portion could be safely clipped off into the small box attached to the snuffer causing the flame to continue to burn brightly. Some pairs of snuffers are extremely sophisticated and beautifully fashioned. Most are of steel but

Victorian stone spirit jars and glass beer and lemonade bottles, 1880–1910. The small wooden implement was used to open the glass marble-sealed lemonade bottles of the period

japanned snuffers exist as well as rare examples found in silver (see page 21) and even gold.

SCRATCHERS Turned wood long-handled sticks terminating in a carved hand of bone or ivory, the fingers crooked, are well known as back scratchers dating from the 18th and 19th centuries. More rare are the similar objects with straight fingers, which were for searching up under the wig in order to scratch the head.

SOVEREIGN SCALES These delicate, fascinating little scales, easily carried in the pocket, folded flat into slim metal or wooden cases and are less than 15cm (6in) in length. They were used by shopkeepers, travellers and money changers, particularly in harbour areas where there was foreign trade. They helped to eradicate the circulation of forgeries in gold coin.

JELLY MOULDS Moulds in copper and pottery are still to be obtained, although modern copies have been made. The superb copper jelly moulds were a feature of the *batterie de cuisine*, such an essential element in the furnishing of any great 18th- or early 19th-century kitchen. An excellent example are the moulds at The Royal Pavilion, Brighton, and which are marked with the initials of the great Duke of Wellington.

After 1880 the jelly and blancmange manufacturers began using moulds to advertise their products. The patterns in moulds are many, but the first and most sophisticated were the painted moulds made by Wedgwood during the 18th century. They were made of the cream pottery known as Queensware and various pyramid, wedge, and obelisk shapes were used. The moulds are in two sections – the inner hand-painted floral mould and its outer case. When the jelly had set the outer case was removed and the hand-painted pottery shapes in the centre of the calves-foot jelly could clearly be seen.

SKILLETS Bronze cauldrons were used in Britain from very early times and through the 19th century. It was the development of new stoves and kitchen ranges that rendered them obsolete at last. Genuine bronze examples dating from the 16th or 17th centuries are rare and valuable but Victorian cast-iron cauldrons are by no means to be dismissed. They retained the old cauldron shape and the casting seams on the outside are easily seen.

Skillets are also early cooking vessels and were in use during the 14th century, made of bronze or bell metal. They are a form of early saucepan complete with handle. Very early examples have a narrow top bellying out towards the bottom. When the skillet is a more formal saucepan shape and mounted on three legs they are from a later period. Such utensils are becoming increasingly scarce but the skillet is a fine object and very desirable. During the 18th century they went out of use because the interiors of these vessels were usually tinned and the tinning was seldom done well. When worn through, corruptions occurred in the metal causing food poisoning, and even in those days people realized it probably originated from dirty, badly tinned utensils. Some skillets have the maker's name cast in the handle, and it is not uncommon for them to have brief texts cast in the handle in the same manner.

Horse brasses and rural bygones

With the coming of each season the Victorian farmworker was called upon to turn his hand to many skills. Hedging, ditching, ploughing, threshing – all required an understanding of the living landscape and its creatures, of the crops planted and of the animals worked and reared. They used all manner of hand tools that had changed but little over centuries. Sickles and scythes, flails, faghooks, turnip picks and sheep shears. There were wooden rattles and clappers for scaring birds from crops, and revolving wooden lures set with small mirrors to entice larks to the gun.

The tools of the old animal doctors, who continued to work until 1948 in Britain when it became law that only the professionally qualified could practise veterinary medicine, are full of interest. Scores of different types of horseshoes are to be found at country markets and, indeed, in the fields themselves. From Roman times to the 20th century all periods used distinctive shapes of horseshoe which can be identified. Farm buildings provide the perfect setting for collections of this nature, but a few carefully chosen rural bygones can add character and interest to any house.

Horse brasses

Most people will recognize a horse brass when they see one, although deciding whether or not it is old or new may present them with a little more difficulty. Anyone who begins to take a deeper interest in the subject will soon master the various methods of manufacture, recognize the symbolism of the many designs, and come to differentiate between the rare, unusual and mere commonplace.

The history of the horse brass is a long one, having its roots in superstitition, fear of the unknown, and an awareness of natural forces whether destructive or benign. From the Bible we know that Gideon collected ornaments from the necks of camels he captured from enemies. Such was the beginning of the use of amulets to ward off the evil eye from cattle and the animals that carried man. The Crusaders returned from their journeys and battles, with decorative horse trappings as part of the spoils of war. In medieval days horses wore plumes for tournament and on the battlefield. Such plumes remained popular with the coming of the Industrial Revolution that was to see the development of the horse brass as we know them today. The wives of ploughmen and carters created a tradition of making ear-covers decorated with stitched patterns and tufts of wool for their husbands' horse teams.

Following World War II the heavy horse was quickly supplanted by the tractor, to such an extent that as well as becoming rare they became in danger of extinction. During the past decade this dangerous situation has been halted and reversed. New heavy-horse societies flourish, and ploughing matches have again become part of rural life. Horse brasses have always looked well decorating black beams or a fine brick fireplace, but they look even better when part of the 'turn-out' of a giant horse standing 17 hands high and weighing over 1015kg (1 ton)! So much has interest increased in such horses and their brasses that, in 1976, The National Horse Brass Society was formed.

Among the earliest motifs seen on brasses are many designs from nature, the sun and the moon, hearts and stars, animals and sheaves of corn. Trappings for the horses that pulled royal coaches and the conveyances of the nobility often carried decorations of heraldic arms, crests and ciphers in silver gilt, silver, or silver plate. It may well be that such a practice further encouraged humbler folk to make similar ornaments in a more base metal with designs of their own imagination.

The collector today can still find horse brasses dating back to the early years of the reign of Queen Victoria but they do grow increasingly scarce. The Golden and Diamond Jubilees of Queen Victoria were occasions that produced many commemorative brasses, as too did her death in 1901. As invariably happens when any class of object becomes popular, copies are made. Dates on brasses should not be taken at face value, and many copies were manufactured after World War II when brass again became readily available. It has been estimated that some two dozen different designs of horse brass were made to mark our present Queen's Silver Jubilee in 1977, and this type of modern brass should certainly not be ignored by collectors.

Heavy horses at a ploughing match display the traditional glory of their brass trappings and embroidered ear-covers. Note the crescent face pieces and the brass bedecked martingales

Many horse brasses could have been made by the men who worked the horses, cutting the brasses by hand from sheets of flat brass. Punch, hammer, chisel and file would have been the tools used but, again, hammer marks may be added to a brass at any period by the unscrupulous. Designs stamped from sheet brass can be old, for machinery was introduced for such work in about 1880. Cast brass was a production technique used from about 1825. Casting had the advantages of cheapness and the ability to produce any number of a required design quickly. The creation of more intricate patterns also made casting popular and this method of production being cheaper, is of course, still in use today.

Brass varies considerably in quality depending upon the proportions of ingredients used, copper and zinc forming the major part. Other metals that might be added include lead, tin and iron. For casting it is necessary to have a mould, the patterns of which were carved in close-grain pearwood from which the sand mould was made ready to take the molten brass. The brass was then cleaned off by hand, taking off any rough edges and giving the brass a polish before dispatch. Many of these brasses have two prominent studs on the reverse, one on each side of the brass. These studs were cast in order to hold the brass in a vice for its final finish. Often the studs were filed off but even so some trace of them can usually be felt and seen.

Modern brasses copying old designs are seldom so well finished as their earlier counterparts, neither does modern brass tend to hold its polish for so long. Although fakes do exist it would be true to say that most modern brasses do not pretend to be anything other than what they are.

The basic complement of brasses for a heavy horse is as follows:

Face Brass one or more brasses over the forehead and sometimes hanging between the eyes.
Ear Brasses simple brasses behind each ear.
Breast-Piece or Martingale Brasses the strap fastened from the collar to the girth may carry up to ten brasses. This strap frequently carries the finest brasses.
Runner Brasses three brasses at each shoulder.
Loin Brasses seldom used on a working harness, but a series of short straps used to carry extra decoration on special occasions.
Fly Terret or Swinger This consists of a flat miniature disc or bell, plain or decorated, swinging in a frame over the head of the horse. The frame screwed into the leather of the lead-strap. As the disc or bell swung with the movement of the animal's head it also had the effect of helping to discourage flies. Some of the best examples are fitted with small brush-like plumes in red, white and blue. Fly terrets should always be obtained when the price is felt to be reasonable, for they are no longer easy to find.

Horses brasses such as those listed might easily produce a combined weight of 4.5kg (10lb) or more, according to the number of loin straps.

Brasses fall into a number of categories. It was the Romany Gipsy who introduced the 'card patterns' of clubs and diamonds that are occasionally seen. Travelling tinkers frequently turned their skills to brasses and were responsible for producing that one group of brasses that have moving parts. A brass star with another that revolves superimposed is typical of this type.

Now much collected are the R.S.P.C.A. merit brasses, once awarded at ploughing matches and shows. Not surprisingly it is such documentary brasses as these that are among the most interesting, bearing as they do the dates and names of horse shows, and the once common parades of van and cart horses.

Brasses with estate crests are also well worth seeking, as are all those associated with trade and industry. Anchors, capstans and sailing ships were much favoured by carters working among the docks, just as the railway carters were proud to display brasses with engines. The butcher's brass was an ox, the miller's a windmill, the brewery drays sported brass barrels. Peacock brasses were frequently worn by brood mares for this splendid bird was the sacred symbol of Hera, the Greek goddess of fertility.

Portrait brasses ranging from royalty and generals to sportsmen, poets and politicians tend to be modern but not at all unworthy of collecting. Above all, it is perhaps the brasses that portray the horse that have a permanent place in the affections of most. So too are all the designs associated with the soil and harvest, the wheatsheaves and the acorns. Among the most common, yet important to any collection of horse brasses are the crescents and the sun discs; constant reminders of the origin of horse brasses steeped in superstition and the reality of the rhythm of the passing of the months and seasons.

Bells

The history of the bell has been, and continues to be, the subject of many scholarly monographs. So far as we are now concerned with the collectable trappings of the horse, there are two types of bell of particular interest.

◪ LATTEN BELLS are the aristocrats among horse bells and always much prized by their owners. Daniel Defoe refers to such bells in his journal of a tour through England in the early 18th century, but the best account of them comes from the pen of Gertrude Jekyll in her book *Old West Surrey* published in 1904. Miss Jekyll is now celebrated as one of the great gardeners and garden designers of the Victorian era, and she also possessed a clear eye for social change and country matters. Here she describes the latten bells worn by a team of horses: 'There were four rings of bells in the set, and each set had four bells, except the one with three of the largest bells of deep tone; each set made its own chord, while the whole changed and jingled in pleasant harmonies. The leather hood was often scalloped or evenly jagged at the lower edge, and generally had a pretty running ornament of barley, incised with a small gouge in the surface of the leather. A red woollen fringe hunge inside the hood; sometimes it came only a little way down, but generally was so long as to hide the bells completely. The two spikes passed down the two sides of the collar along the hames.

The original use of the bells on the harness was to give notice in the narrow lanes, so that a carter hearing a distant team, could either wait before entering the lane, or draw to the side in good time at some wider part. There is a legend of two carters who purposely ignored the warning, met in the middle of the narrow lane, and fought the matter out. How the battle ended and how the teams and wagons were got out remains unrecorded in local history.'

Brass-cased hame (see the illustration on p. 75), six 19th-century horse brasses and a rumbler bell with the initials of Robert Wells (1764–1825)

That most vivid account of the bells and their use is enough to whet the appetite of almost any collector in this particular field. Although Miss Jekyll described various forms of decoration on or attached to the leather hood of latten bells, many sets are seen entirely plain.

The second kind of bell under discussion here is spherical and known as a 'crotal'.

◪ CROTAL BELLS Often described as 'rumbler bells' they contain a metal ball that causes the bell to ring at every movement of the horse. They were made in a number of sizes ranging from small sheep bells to crotals measuring 11.5cm ($4\frac{1}{2}$in) in diameter. The underside has a broad mouth-like opening, and there are four round holes in the top of the sphere surrounding the cast loop for hanging. The large bells tended not to be worn by waggon horses, but by fire-engine horses and cab-horses. The smaller horse bells were frequently hung in sets of four from the headband. An engraving by Albrecht Dürer of 1515 depicts horses hung with many crotal bells.

Many bells bear the cast initials of their makers,

Horse-bits were made to suit horses carrying out particular roles, as well as to deal with individual temperaments. This photograph shows just some of the shapes to be found

and one of those most often found is R. W. The initials are those of Robert Wells (1764–1825), one of the finest bell founders of the 18th century.

Horse bits and yokes

HORSE BITS All harness and trappings associated with horses, particularly the coach horse and the great heavy breeds of working horses, are now collected and even odd leathers or blinkers carrying brass, pewter, or other base metal studs are much sought after. A vital part of the harness, yet so often overlooked by many collectors are horse bits. The variations in the design of bits are remarkable for they were made to suit horses carrying out particular tasks or to cope with a horse of special temperament or habits. There were bits made for soft-mouthed horses and others for breaking-in. Coaching bits with such names as 'Pelham' or 'Buxton', although highly practical, are also minor works of art with their swirling curves and loops. Some bits are detachable on one side so that a horse could feed while still in the shafts. Bits bearing the makers' names are always interesting for they provide important additional information and may also enable a bit to be accurately dated.

YOKES Shoulder yokes for the carrying of two pails of milk or water are not only decorative but firmly remind us of the hard physical work once the lot of women working in the dairy or fetching water from well to house. Many different woods were used for making yokes but willow was preferred due to its lightness.

Craft tools

The hand tools of the traditional craftsmen from farriers, blacksmiths and wheelwrights, to carpenters, leatherworkers and shipwrights, are frequently beautiful in terms of shape as well as curiosity. Fine examples from the 18th and 19th centuries are now in great demand as more people have come to appreciate their quality and the scope they offer, and so well demonstrated in the accompanying photograph. Many tools carry the names of the firms or individuals who made them; some also have the names or initials of the craftsmen who used them. Where addresses are included in the marks, opportunity is provided

Farm workers harvest barrel, horn beakers, a wetstone holder *(top left)*, cowhorn straightner *(centre)*, a billhook and four shepherds crooks showing varying regional styles

19th-century craft tools, including a leather worker's mallet and a sewing clamp, woodworking planes and a shipwright's caulking mallet

Single-barrel side action 12 bore hammer gun by G. E. Lewis, Lower Loveday Street, Birmingham, 19th century

for further research in the 19th-century trade catalogues or directories, and this can lead in some cases to the reconstruction of the history of a tool from its manufacture to its subsequent user.

Shotguns

The type of gun mentioned here is not the costly, finely-chased hand-made weapon of the sportsman, but the workaday tool of the gamekeeper, tenant farmer, and cottager used to control vermin and shoot rabbits for the pot. All fine guns and the muzzle-loading weapons of the 18th century are now costly, but the 19th-century guns may still be obtained reasonably from time to time. Guns of this type, often the work of Birmingham gunmakers, have much character and look well when hung above a stone fireplace or against an old beam. Guns that require extensive restoration are not worth buying unless they can be obtained cheaply. Old double-barrelled hammer guns are well worth buying for they will almost certainly become increasingly collected. Single-barrelled side-hammer weapons are particularly attractive, and the early pin-fire weapons are certain to become collectors' items, as are the large-bore wildfowling guns. The breech-loading gun developed from the drop-down barrel weapon exhibited at the Great Exhibition of 1851 by a French gunmaker named Lefancheux, which fired cartridges detonated by a projecting brass pin. During the 1850s and sixties a battle raged between the advocates of the percussion muzzle loader and those for the new-fangled breach loader; muzzle loaders continued to be made through the 1860s.

Purchasers of shotguns in Britain require a shotgun licence if the gun is able to be fired.

Bibliography

General

BRIDGEMAN, Harriet, and DRURY, Elizabeth (Edited by), *The Encyclopedia of Victoriana*, Country Life, 1975

MURRAY, Peter and Linda, *A Dictionary of Art and Artists*, Penguin, 1959

OSBORNE, Harold (Editor), *The Oxford Companion to the Decorative Arts*, Oxford University Press, 1975

Porcelain and pottery

COYSH, A. W., *Blue and Whjte Transfer Ware 1780–1840*, David & Charles, 1970

COYSH, A. W., *British Art Pottery*, David & Charles, 1976

GODDEN, G. A., *British Porcelain, an Illustrated Guide*, Barrie & Jenkins, 1974

GODDEN, G. A., *British Pottery, an Illustrated Guide*, Barrie & Jenkins, 1974

PRICE, Bernard, *The Arthur Negus Guide to English Pottery and Porcelain*, Hamlyn, 1978

PUGH, P. D. Gordon, *Staffordshire Portrait Figures*, Praeger Publishers, Inc. New York, 1971 (distributed by TABS in the UK)

SAVAGE, George, and NEWMAN, Harold, *An Illustrated Dictionary of Ceramics*, Thames and Hudson, 1974

TAIT, Hugh, *Porcelain*, Hamlyn, 1972

Glass

WEBBER, Norman W., *Collecting Glass*, David & Charles, 1972

WILLS, Geoffrey, *Victorian Glass*, G. Bell & Sons, 1976

Silver

Pocket books of hallmarks on silver are obtainable from many antique shops and jewellers, as well as book shops.

DE CASTRES, Elizabeth, *A Guide to Collecting Silver*, Queen Anne Press, Macdonald Futura Publishers, 1980

INGLIS, Brand, *The Arthur Negus Guide to British Silver*, Hamlyn, 1980

Paintings, prints, maps and needlework

LEWIS, Charles T. C., *George Baxter, His Life and Work*, 1908 (Reprinted by E. P. Publishing, 1972)

HODGKISS, Alan G., *Discovering Antique Maps*, Shire Publications, 1975

BANKS, Steven, *The Handicrafts of The Sailor*, David & Charles, 1974

KENDRICK, A. F., *English Needlework*, A. & C. Black, 1933

KING, Donald, *Samplers*, Victoria and Albert Museum, HMSO, 1960

Stevengraphs, postcards and cards

GODDEN, G. A., *Stevengraphs and Other Victorian Silk Pictures*, Barry & Jenkins, 1971

BYATT, Anthony, *Picture Postcards and Their Publishers*, Golden Age Postcard Books, 1978

Books and photographs

McLEAN, Ruari, *Victorian Book Design and Colour Printing*, Faber & Faber, 1963 (Second edition, enlarged and revised, 1972)

WITKIN, Lee D., and LONDON, Barbara, *The Photograph Collectors Guide*, Secker and Warburg, 1979

Jewellery

AUSTEN, R. L. *Gems and Jewels*, Evans Brothers, 1979

FALKINER, Richard, *Investing In Antique Jewellery*, Barrie & Rockliff, 1968

HINKS, Peter, *Jewellery*, Hamlyn, 1969

Coins and tokens

PRICE, M. J., *Coins*, Hamlyn in association with British Museum Publications, 1980

Toys

COLEMAN, Dorothy S., Elizabeth A., and Evelyn J., *The Collectors Encyclopedia of Dolls*, Crown Publishers Inc., New York, 1968 (distributed by Thomas Nelson in the UK)

MACKAY, James, *Nursery Antiques*, Ward Lock, 1976

Metalwork

HORNSBY, Peter, *The Arthur Negus Guide to Pewter and Brass*, Hamlyn 1981

PEAL, Christopher A., *British Pewter & Britannia Metal*, John Gifford, 1971

Domestic and rural bygones

There are many booklets dealing with craft tools, bygones, etc. published by Shire Publications.

Acknowledgments

The publishers would like to thank the following:

Bayly's Gallery, London: 33, 35 (below), 41 (both)
Baynton-Williams, London: 32 (below)
By courtesy of Birmingham Museums and Art Gallery: 71 (centre)
J. H. Bourdon-Smith Ltd, London: title-page, 18, 19, 21, 23, 24, 26
Photo David Bradfield, London: front jacket
Cameo Corner, Liberty & Co. Ltd, London: 52, 54, 55, (all), 56 (all)
Jack Casimir Ltd, London: 64, 65
Castle Museum, Norwich (Photo Gerry Yardy): 70, 71 (below)
Cooper-Bridgeman Library, London: 62, 63 (right)
Photo S. Eost, London: 32 (above)
Geoffrey Godden Collection: 9 (right)
Messrs Godden of Worthing Ltd: half-title, 7, 8, 9 (left), 10, 11 (Magna Carta plate and pot lids), 11 (below), 12, 13, 36, 37, 38, 59 (below – Sussex pot), 66 (pewter mug)
Photo C. Howard & Son Ltd, Chichester: 28, 29 (above), 30 (left)
Melvyn Jay Antiques, London: 67
Eric Lineham, London: 15 (Burmese glass), 16 (except Mary Gregory and Sowerby glass)
The Mander and Mitchenson Theatre Collection, London: 10, 17, 22, 25, 27, 30 (right), 30 (both), 42 (above), 42 (left), 51, 58 (left)
Pollock's Toy Museum, London: 63 (below)
Photo E. Richardson, London: 10, 17, 22, 25, 27, 29 (Baxter), 30 (both), 42 (left), 51, 58 (left)
Collection Robert Sharman, London, 61 (pilgrim badge)
Maureen Thompson, London: 14, 15 (except Burmese glass), 16 (Mary Gregory and Sowerby glass)
Victoria and Albert Museum, London: 32 (above)
Photo Lee Weatherley, East Grinstead, Sussex: 75
William Whelan Ltd, London: 59 (below right)
Photo Derrick Witty, Wraysbury, Staines, Middx: back of jacket, title-page, 7, 8, 9, 10, 11 (both), 12, 13, 14, 15, 16, 18, 19, 21, 23, 24, 26, 29 (below), 32 (below), 33, 34, 35 (both), 37 (3 portraits), 39, 43, 44, 45 (all), 46, 47, 48, 50 (both), 52, 55 (all), 56 (all), 58 (below left and right), 59 (below), 59 (below right), 60 (both), 61, 64, 65, 66, 67, 68, 71 (above), 73, 76, 77 (both), 78 (both)

Index

Figures in **bold** type refer to illustrations

ale warmers **64**, 65
amber **54–5**
Amberina glass **16**, 17
ampullae 61
apostle spoon 23
Art Nouveau
  glass **16**, 17
  pewter **66**
Art Union 9, 42
asparagus servers 25, **26**
assay offices 18, 19, 20
Attwell, Mabel Lucy, **39**
Augustus Rex monogram 7

Bartolozzi **32**
Bateman family (silversmiths) 24–5
Baxter, George, **30**, 47
Beardsley, Aubrey, **45**
beleek porcelain brooches 55
bells, horse, **76–7**
Berlin iron jewellery **55**
Berlin woolwork **33**
Biedermeier 63
Billies and Charlies **59–60**
birthstones 57
bog-oak jewellery **45**
bookbindings (Victorian) **44–5**, 48, 49
bookmarkers
  silk, **1**, 36, 37, **38**, 41
  silver 27
books **44–9**
  gift 45
  prize **48–9**
  Victorian illustrated 45–7
bottles **73**
bottle tickets *see* wine labels
Boulton, Matthew, 20, 56, 67
boxes, silver, **27**
brass **64–5**
brasses, horse, **74–6**
bread boards 69
bright cutting 23, **24**
Bristol blue glass **15**, 17
Britannia metal **64**, 66–7
Britannia silver **18–19**
Burmese glass **15**, 16–17
butter pats and prints **68**, 69

caddy spoons **24**
cameo glass 17
cameos 54
Cameron, Julia Margaret, 49
candle
  extinguishers **72**
  snuffers **21**, **69**, 72–3
  sticks 65
card cases 26–7
carnival glass 17
cartes-de-visite **50**, 51
carver rests 26
carving sets 25
cased glass *see* flashed glass
Caughley 8, 10, **12**
'ceramic pastry' 70
ceramics 6–14
chestnut roaster **65**
Chinese porcelain 6, 7, 12–**13**
Ch'ing Dynasty 13
chinoiserie 12
Christmas cards 41–2
chromolithography 30, 32, 42, 43, **46**, 47
Coalport **8**
coins **58**
  clipping of, 18–19
Cole, Henry, 41–2
colour printing 30, 32, 45, 46–7
commemorative
  china **10**
  medals **58**
  playing cards 43
copper **64–5**
coral jewellery 54
cranberry glass 14–**15**
Crane, Walter **41**
crotal bells 76
cups and saucers **8**, 12
  armorial **13**
  large size **70**
cut-steel jewellery **56**
Cynicus 39

dating
  of porcelain 7, 13
  of silver 19
Derby **8**
Dobbs, H. 40, **41**
dolls 62, **63**
Dresden 7, 63
  Crown **7**

Eaton, Charles 59–60
electroplate 67
embroidery 33–5
engraving 31–2
  on glass 14–15
  on silver 22
engravings 30, **31–2**
  aquatint 31, 46
etchings 30, 31

fairy lamps **15**, 16
fenders, brass 65
fire irons 65
fish slices **2**, 25
flashed glass **16**, 17
flat irons 69–70
footwarmer **69**
forks 25
fossil jewellery **52**, **53**
Foster, Birket **47**
Fox Talbot, W. H. 49, 51

Gallé, Emile 17
game pie dishes 70
Gill, Eric 29, **30**
glass 14–17
glasses, drinking **14**–15
Grant, W.H. 37, 40
grape scissors 25, **26**
guns 78

hair jewellery **52**
hallmarks, silver **18**, **19**–20, 21–2, 25, 66
  on spoons 23, 24
  transposed 22
hand warmers 71
horn beakers 69, **77**
horse trappings 74–7
Humphreys, Henry Noel **46–7**

illustration, book 45–7
  photographic 49
Imari ware 12–13
iron jewellery **55**
irons **69**–70
ironstone 8, **9**
ivory 53

Jacobite glasses 15
Jacquard, Joseph 36, 38
Japanese porcelain 6, 12–**13**
jars
  spirit **73**
  storage **68**, 69
jelly moulds 73
jet **52**, 53
jettons **60–1**
jewellery 52–7

knitting sheaths 70–1
knife
  cleaners 68–9
  rests 26
knives 25, **26**, 68, 69

ladles **2**, 25
Lalique glass **16**
lamps, brass 65
latten bells 76
lava cameos **54**
Leach,
  Bernard 11
  David **11**
Leighton,
  George 47
  John 42, 45, 47
linen polishers **70**, 71
lithography 30, **31**, 46

maps **32–3**
Marigold glass 17
marks
  on glass 15, 17
  plate 31
  pontil 15
  on porcelain 7, 10, 13
  on silver **18**, **19**–20, 21–2, 23, 24, 66
  touch 66
Mary Gregory glass **16**
Mason's Ironstone 8, **9**
Mauchline Ware 72
medals, commemorative **58**
Meissen 6, 7
mezzotints 31
Minton **8**, **9**
mosaic jewellery 54, **55**
mote-skimmer 24
muff warmers **71**
music covers 30–1

Nailsea glass **15**, 17
napkin rings **26**
Nuremberg jettons 60–1

Ogilvy, John **32**, 33
oil paintings **28–9**
Oriental ceramics 6, 7, 12–**13**

Parian ware, 8, **9**, 63
paste jewellery **56**
pestles and mortars 69
pewter **66**
photographs 39–40, 49–51
  as book illustrations 49
pictures 28–32
pilgrim badges 60, **61**
pinchbeck **56**
pin cushions 27, 70, 72
playing cards 42–3
pontil mark 15
porcelain 6–14
postcards 38–40, 51
posy holder 22
pot lids **9**, **11**
pottery 6, 7, 9, 11–13
Pratt & Co., F. & R. 9, 11
pressed glass **16**, **17**
prints 30, 31–2
  Baxter 30, 47

quill cutters **71**

Ravenscroft glass 14
rings **57**
  mourning 52–3, 57
rolling pins 69
Royal Doulton 8

samplers **35**
Samson et Cie 8
Saxton, Christopher 33
school prize books **48–9**
scoops **2**, 25
scratchers, back **72**, 73
scratch-weight 22
Sèvres 6, 7–8
Sheffield plate **67**
shell cameos **54**
ship embroideries **34–5**
shotguns **78**
silk-woven
  bookmarkers **1**, 36, 37, **38**, 41
  pictures **36–8**
  postcards 40
  valentines 41
silver 18–27, 67
  alterations to 22
  coins 58
  foreign 20
  nickel 67
  standards 18–19
skewers, silver **2**, 25
skillets **65**, 73
skimmer
  copper **68**
  mote 24
skirt holders **71**
slag glass 17
Smith brothers (painters) 29
Smith, William 59–60
snuff boxes **27**, 72
soldiers, toy **62–3**
sovereign scales **71**, 73
Spode 8, 10, **70**
spoons **2**, **21**, **23**–5, **26**
Staffordshire figures 9, **10**
Sterling silver 18–19
Stevengraphs **36–8**
Stevens, Thomas 36–**8**, 40, 41, 42, **45**
stoneware 11
  celadon 12
  spirit jars **73**
  storage jars **68**, 69
  warmers **69**, **71**
sugar
  cutters **68**, 72
  tongs 25, **26**

Tarot cards 43
tea caddies **18**, 23–4
tea drinking 12, 24
tobacco boxes 27, **72**
tokens
  hop **59**
  trade **58**
tools
  craft 77, **78**
  farm 74, **77**
toys **62–3**
transfer printing 9
transfer ware **10**, **11**
treen 72
trivets 65
'Tudric' ware **66**

valentine cards 40–1
vesta boxes **27**
vinaigrettes **27**

Wallace, James **29**
warming pans 64–5
watercolours **28**, 29–30
Wedgwood **11**, 69, 70, 73
Whitby jet **52**, 53
Wilson, Stanley **28**, 29
wine labels 26, **27**
woolwork
  Berlin 33
  pictures **34–5**

yokes 77
York Exhibition, 1879, 36, 38